THE HISTORY OF
SCOTLAND
FOR CHILDREN

LOMOND

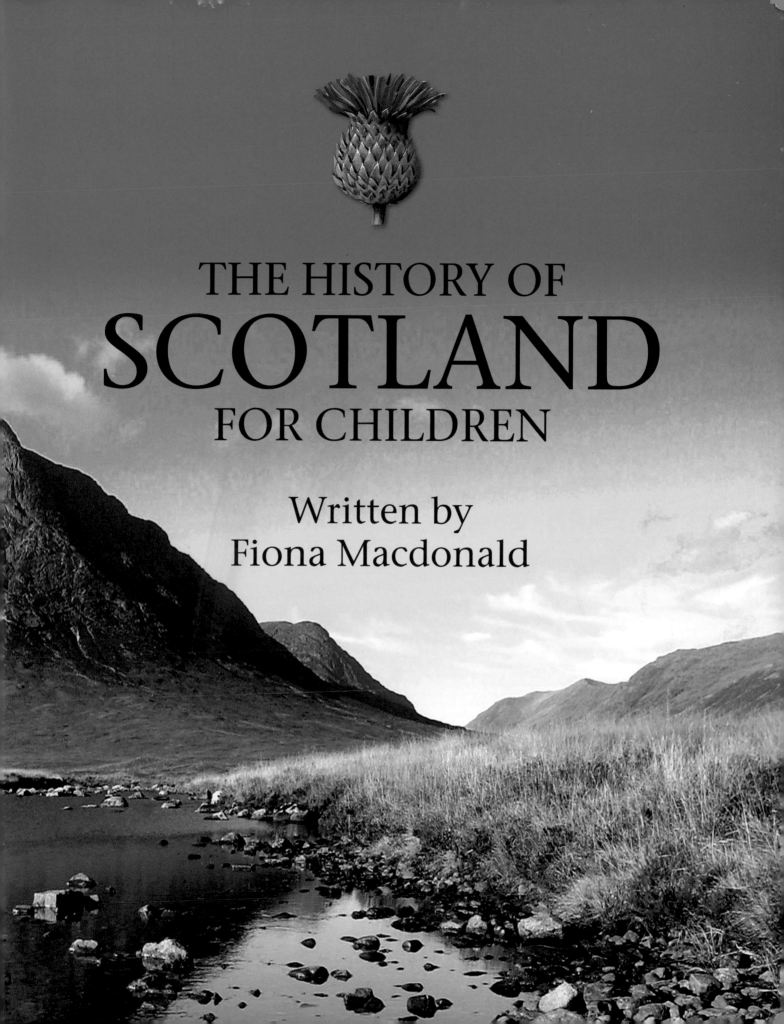

THE HISTORY OF
SCOTLAND
FOR CHILDREN

Written by
Fiona Macdonald

This edition published for
Lomond Books Ltd, Broxburn,
EH52 5NF, Scotland. 2011
www.lomondbooks.com

ISBN 978-1-84204-073-7

Printed in China

Written by Fiona Macdonald

Project manager/Photo
researcher: Vicci Parr
Designer: Fiona Grant
Consultant: Brian Williams

Contents

Stone circle at
Calanais, Lewis

Vikings arrive
from Norway

Ancient Scotland,
10,000BC to 1745

Bonnie Prince Charlie
escapes with
Flora MacDonald

Early shelters
known as brochs

Macbeth fights
Duncan for
the throne

Massacre of the
MacDonalds at
Glencoe

Highlanders
drive cattle to
Lowland
markets

Scottish kings are
crowned at Scone

Early
settlers

Abbey at Iona –
founded by
St Columba

William Wallace
leads Scots
at Stirling Bridge

Mary Queen
of Scots
imprisoned

Lords of
the Isles

Elegant 18th-century
Edinburgh

Norman-style
castles

James II obtains
new guns

Hadrian's
Wall

  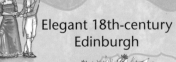   

Modern Scotland, 1745 to Present

ISLE OF LEWIS

SKYE

Highland clearances of crofters

INVERNESS

Highland tourism increases

Wildlife conservation becomes popular

Films shot on location

Balmoral, holiday home of Queen Victoria

ABERDEEN

Oil found off east coast

Highland traditions revive

DUNDEE

MULL

Railways and heavy industry

PERTH

Coal mining

GLASGOW

Forth Rail Bridge

Nuclear submarine bases

EDINBURGH

ISLAY

High-rise housing replaces slums

New building for Scottish Parliament

Scots emigrate to America

Hunger marches from Scotland to England

NORTHERN IRELAND

ENGLAND

Ancient Scotland

In the first 6,000 years of its history, Scotland became
home to hunters, gatherers, raiders, invaders, farmers,
craftworkers, missionaries, warlords and kings.
Scottish people created huge monuments,
clever technologies and many wonderful works
of art that we can still admire today.

After the Ice

Scotland was one of the last places in Europe where people settled. Scotland remained empty for so long because, when modern humans first moved out of Africa and began to spread around the world over 50,000 years ago, it was mostly covered by ice.

Then, the world's weather was much colder than it is today. Northern Europe, North America and northern Asia were covered by glaciers – massive ice-sheets up to 100 metres (330 feet) thick – and large areas of sea-bed were left uncovered, creating "bridges" of dry land. Scientists and historians call these freezing years "Ice Ages".

Scotland's first settlers lived in groups of around 10 or 12 people. Men, women and children all worked together to survive, but life was hard and few reached more than 40 years old.

Animals arrive

The last Ice Age began around 70,000BC and reached its peak around 18,000BC. But slowly, over the centuries, the world's weather grew warmer. The glaciers melted and by around 10,000BC Scotland was free from ice. Trees and bushes began to grow, and animals such as bears, wolves and wild pigs came searching for food.

Summer visitors

The first people to set foot in Scotland arrived soon afterwards on summer hunting expeditions. They travelled over land bridges or in boats (made from hollowed-out logs) from Ireland, Germany and further south in the British Isles. But the weather was still very cold and they went away in wintertime.

The first settlers

However, the weather went on getting warmer and around 9000BC some hunters decided to stay. They built tents of animal skins, and shelters of tree branches and brushwood. They hunted wild animals, caught fish and gathered fruits and berries. They made tools from wood, antler, stone and bone. They preserved meat for winter by smoking it over wood fires.

Nomad lives

These hunters and gatherers lived as nomads, moving their camps from place to place according to the seasons to get the best shelter and to find the most food. They also used boats to explore the coasts and venture inland along lochs and rivers. By around 7000BC they had spread to most parts of the country. Scotland's first settlers had arrived!

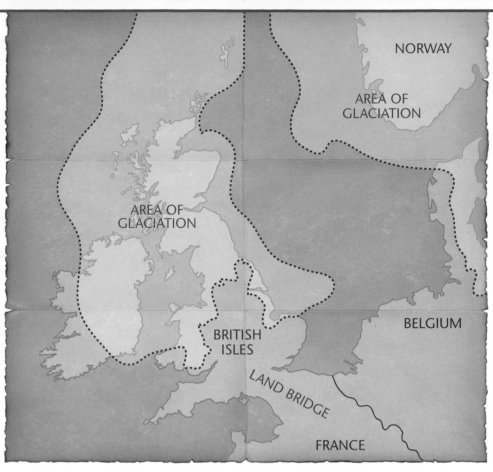

The British Isles around 18,000BC. The northern half was covered by glaciers. The south and east were joined to the rest of Europe by a land bridge.

Did you know?
The years from around 10,000BC to 5000BC in Scotland are known as the "Mesolithic", or "Middle Stone Age", era.

These pieces of stone, found at the site of a hunters' camp, date from around 8000–5000BC. They were left over from making stone tools.

Settlers Start to Arrive

around 70,000BC	**around 35,000BC**	**around 10,000BC**	**around 9000BC**	**around 8500BC**	**around 7000BC**
Start of last Ice Age; Scotland covered by ice.	First modern humans arrive in (south) British Isles.	End of Ice Age; Scotland no longer ice covered.	First hunters and gatherers arrive in Scotland.	Sea-levels rise, land bridges flooded. British Isles cut off from rest of Europe.	By now, hunters and gatherers have settled all over Scotland.

The First Farmers

Around 4000BC, hunters in Scotland stopped living as nomads. They built settled communities with permanent houses on fertile, low-lying land around the coast. They still went hunting and fishing but produced most of their food by farming.

These first farmers reared sheep, cattle, pigs and goats to provide meat, milk, skins and wool. They made hay by cutting dry grass in summertime to feed their animals in winter. Using stone axes, they cleared the land of trees and bushes. They protected it with fences and walls, then planted seeds of oats and barley each autumn. In summer when the crops were ripe they cut them down, threshed (beat) them to shake out the grains, dried these over an open fire and stored them to eat later.

Scotland's first farmers relied on tools like this stone axe with a wooden handle.

Early farmers built huge timber houses for shelter, and to store their food and possessions.

Survival skills

By storing food such as grain, families now had a much better chance of surviving Scotland's harsh winters. By staying in one place they had the time to build stronger, larger, more comfortable homes instead of temporary shelters.

Their new homes had space to store food and new possessions such as pottery bowls, stone troughs and wooden buckets. These were stronger than lightweight containers used by nomads, such as woven baskets, and preserved their contents more securely.

Slow change

This change of lifestyle from hunting to farming did not happen suddenly. It developed slowly over hundreds of years. Knowledge of farming techniques may have been carried to Scotland by settlers from further south. Or farming might have developed locally as hunters learned how to encourage wild seeds to grow and how to tame wild animals. Either way, farming brought big changes to the way people lived.

Farming tools

To help manage their land, the first farmers in Scotland also used new tools such as digging sticks and stone hoes to prepare the ground for growing seed. They also made stone querns – grinding machines made of a heavy stone that turned round on top of another bowl-shaped stone. These crushed ripe grains to make flour.

Underground stone houses were built by farmers at Skara Brae in the Orkney Islands between 3000 and 2000BC.

Monuments and Tombs

Farming communities worked hard but, compared with earlier hunters and gatherers, they had much more time to think, make plans and build massive monuments.

The first farmers did not use writing so we do not know for sure what they thought or believed. But they left behind some amazing evidence to give us clues about their hopes, fears and dreams. Between around 4000BC and 2000BC they built wonderful tombs and massive monuments such as circles of standing stones.

Technology and team leaders

These monuments tell us that early farmers were expert builders. They had discovered how to cut, shape and transport huge lumps of rock using only ropes and simple tools of wood and stone. They were also able to plan and organize elaborate construction projects that needed team-work and team leaders. This suggests that farming communities were now led by chiefs who had the wealth and power to give orders and make other people obey them.

Stone circle at Calanais, Lewis.

Homes for the dead

Tombs were designed like houses, with stone-lined rooms deep underground. In the east of Scotland these were covered with barrows (huge mounds of earth); in the west by cairns (pyramid-shaped heaps of stones). This tells us that farming communities honoured their ancestors and wanted to keep their bodies safe after they died. It also suggests that people believed there was life after death.

Underground tomb chambers, like this one at Maes Howe, were built only for chiefs and members of their families.

Early Scottish people may have used stone circles for worship, or to make astronomical observations.

Mysterious meeting-places

Hundreds of tall standing stones (stones raised upright like pillars) still survive in Scotland today. Many are arranged in massive circles. They were probably built to hold religious rituals and as places for people to meet on important occasions. Often they were aligned with the movements of the Sun – its rays shine on them in special ways at mid-summer or mid-winter. This may mean that early farmers worshipped a Sun god.

Did you know?
In 2003 four bodies were found on South Uist in the Outer Hebrides. All had died around 3000BC and had been preserved by removing their organs, then being placed in a peat bog.

Bronze blades made the best cutting and slicing tools invented yet.

Brilliant Bronze

Around 2000BC a revolutionary
new technology reached Scotland.
People learned how to work with
a metal alloy (mixture) called bronze.
It changed their lives.

Bronze is made from two metals, copper and tin.
When heated to very high temperatures they melt,
become liquid and mix together. Bronze-workers
poured this mixture into clay moulds where it cooled
and hardened. (This process is called "casting".)
When completely cold they rubbed the cast object
against hard stone to create a very sharp edge.

New weapons...
Bronze-smiths used this new
technology to make fine
jewellery which could be worn
by powerful people to show
their wealth and status. But
more importantly they also
used it to make improved tools
and weapons, such as axes
and arrowheads.

...New wars

These new weapons became increasingly important after around 1600BC, when life became harder for many people in Scotland. The population had been growing ever since farming began and by now occupied most of the fertile land. But the climate was slowly growing colder and the higher land could no longer be used for farming. Communities had to fight for fields with their neighbours – and the people with the best bronze weapons had the best chance to survive.

Beaker pottery, made between 2500 and 2000BC.

Tin traders

Copper is found in several parts of Scotland but there are no deposits of tin. Early bronze-workers must have learned their new skills, and got the tin or ready-made bronze they needed, from traders living where tin was mined in Cornwall or Spain. Traders travelled to Scotland by boat along the west coast. They bartered (swapped) tin or bronze for valuable items, such as animal skins and furs, and captives who were handed over by local chieftains as slaves.

New ideas

Traders brought new ideas with them as well as new materials. Around 2000BC a new kind of pottery – known as "beakers" – began to be made in Scotland, and some communities began to bury their dead in a different way. Instead of being buried in family graves, individual men and women were laid in pits or stone boxes called "cists". Jewellery and useful goods such as weapons (for men) and weaving equipment (for women) were buried with them.

A Bronze Age burial cist, showing pottery buried with the dead.

Celtic Scotland

From around 1200BC to AD200 Scotland shared in a civilization that flourished throughout Europe. It is known as "Celtic" – a name given to it by ancient Greeks and Romans who fought against Celtic peoples.

The Celts were never a single, united group. Celtic peoples moved into different regions and developed different cultures. But they all spoke closely related languages, used the same advanced metal technology, admired the same artistic styles and shared similar values, ideas and beliefs. Many Celtic peoples also made their living in similar ways as farmers and craftworkers.

A Celtic chieftain's family.

The latest fashions

Weapons, jewels, metalwork and pottery made for these Celtic leaders were carried by travellers and traders to many parts of Europe. Celtic products soon became highly prized, especially by rich and powerful people who asked their own workers to copy them. Powerful people also began to copy Celtic fashions and beliefs. Slowly, these spread to ordinary people.

A wooden statue of a goddess, around 600BC, found in a peat bog.

Druids (Celtic priests) threw valuable goods – and sometimes people – into peat bogs, as offerings to the gods.

Horses and iron swords

Celtic culture first developed in central Europe. Celtic tribal leaders and warriors there rode fine horses and owned iron swords. Their wealth came from running salt-mines and copper-workings, and also through trade. They worshipped goddesses who guarded their homes and brought fertility, and gods who protected their tribe and gave them strength in war.

Scotland's own ideas

Over the years these new Celtic ideas mingled with existing customs to create many local varieties of Celtic civilization. In Scotland, after around 600BC, people stopped copying "outside" Celtic ideas, and created their own Celtic way of life in Scotland.

Did you know?
We know about Celtic peoples because they were described by the Romans, who could read and write.

Celtic Farmers

The Celts were led by chiefs and warriors, but most Celtic people were farmers who lived in small villages or remote, isolated farms.

The Celts made use of new techniques and inventions to farm their land. Instead of digging the ground by hand, they used a heavy wooden plough pulled by oxen to break up the ground before sowing seeds. Often the plough share (the part that digs into the soil) was tipped with tough, strong iron. This allowed the Celts to grow crops on soils that were too heavy for earlier farmers to cultivate.

Marl and manure

To make their crops grow better, Celtic farmers used manure from farm animals or sea-birds. They dug pits to extract marl (lime – a natural soil improver) and spread it on their land. If they lived by the coast they also used seaweed as fertilizer.

Farming festivals

Celtic farmers celebrated the four seasons of the year with festivals. *Samain* (November) was the beginning of the year and the most important. *Imbolc* (February) marked the beginning of spring and new fertility. At *Beltane* (May), the start of summer, farmers lit bonfires so the smoke would kill pests on their livestock. At *Lugnasad* (August), they looked forward to harvest and the season of plenty.

Celtic fishermen sailed in boats called coracles. They were made from thin strips of wood covered with animal hide.

A farming family's roundhouse. Smoke from the central fire escaped through the thatched roof, making the inside smoky but warm and dry.

Roundhouses

Celtic housing styles varied from place to place, depending on the materials that were available locally and on the local weather.

On wild windy coasts and islands, stone houses were stronger and safer but, in sheltered glens, wooden homes were quicker and easier to build.

Whatever the materials, the most common design for Celtic farms was a cluster of roundhouses. Family members lived in the largest house; smaller buildings were used for sheltering animals and storing food. Grain was kept in underground pits to protect it from rats.

Celtic chieftains drove to war on chariots drawn by horses with harnesses and fittings made of iron.

Iron Inventions

Celtic peoples became powerful by using their new technology –
iron-working. They discovered iron was specially suitable
for horse harnesses, chariot fittings and splendid swords.

Iron is found in many places, including Scotland. But unlike copper and tin it does
not occur naturally in a pure, metallic form. Instead it is always combined with other
minerals in rocks known as iron ore. This has to be crushed and heated using wood
or coal until the iron it contains softens and separates from the rock as a spongy mass
called "bloom". (This is called "smelting".) If heated again and then cooled, the best
bits of bloom can be shaped by hammering. (The name for this process is "forging".)
Forged iron becomes much harder than bronze and can be sharpened
on special stones to create an even keener, more dangerous cutting edge.

Iron-working begins

In Europe, iron-working technology first developed around 800BC among Celtic peoples living in a rich, salt-mining region near Hallstatt, in what is now part of Austria. Knowledge of how to smelt and forge iron soon spread to other parts of Celtic Europe and beyond. It reached Scotland between 700 and 400BC.

Status symbols

Iron tools and weapons, especially swords, soon proved to be much better than bronze ones. They became status symbols – all Scottish chiefs and warriors wanted one! A few Scottish fighters also wore iron helmets to protect their head, together with chain-mail armour made of thousands of interlocking iron rings.

Did you know?
Celtic chiefs won praise and fame by leading their warriors on cattle raids, and by fighting to defend their farmers' lands.

A Celtic chief wearing a chain-mail tunic and a magic torc (metal necklace), and carrying a wood-and-leather shield.

Iron axe-heads made in Scotland.

New Homes

Fights for farmland and wars between well-armed Celtic warriors meant that Scotland was becoming a more dangerous place to live. Between 700BC and AD200 many people in Celtic Scotland built stronger homes.

Sometimes they simply surrounded their existing farmhouse with deep ditches, earth ramparts (steep banks) and strong wooden fences. These kept out bandits and raiders but could not withstand a whole army in wartime.

Lake shelters

In lowland Scotland where there were no suitable sites for hill-forts, people built crannogs (lake shelters). These were roundhouses made of wood and thatch, perched on tall wooden poles. They were sited safely out of reach of attackers in the middle of lakes or lochs.

The only ways to reach a crannog were by boat or by walking along a narrow wooden causeway (raised walkway) that was easy to defend.

Safe high places

For extra safety, communities in highland regions built hill-forts, or "duns". These were clusters of houses surrounded by walls and ramparts. They were perched on top of high places such as hilltops, cliffs or rocky crags.

Tall stone towers

Hill-forts and crannogs were sometimes used as permanent homes and sometimes as emergency shelters. But Celtic peoples in north-western Scotland built a third kind of stronghold called a broch, which they used only when danger threatened. A fire for cooking and keeping warm burned in the open space in the centre of the broch, and defenders shot arrows or threw stones at attackers from the top of its walls.

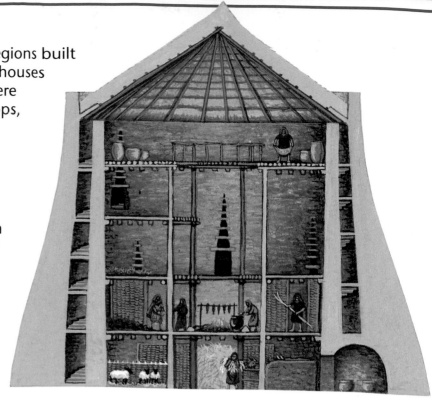

Inside a broch, there were wooden galleries that could be used for storing food and for sleeping. The conical roof was made of thatch.

Brochs were tall, round stone towers with no windows and only a tiny, well-defended door.

Roman Scotland

The Romans ruled the biggest empire the world had ever seen.
At its peak it stretched from Egypt to Germany. In AD43 they landed in
southern Britain. Around AD80 they decided to conquer Scotland as well.

The Roman invasion of Scotland was led by General Agricola in AD81. His troops
marched northwards, building roads so that they could travel quickly, and camps
and forts from which they could control the countryside. Celtic chiefs and warriors
fought back against the invaders but they were no match for the Roman army. In just
two years the Romans conquered most of Scotland south of the River Tay.

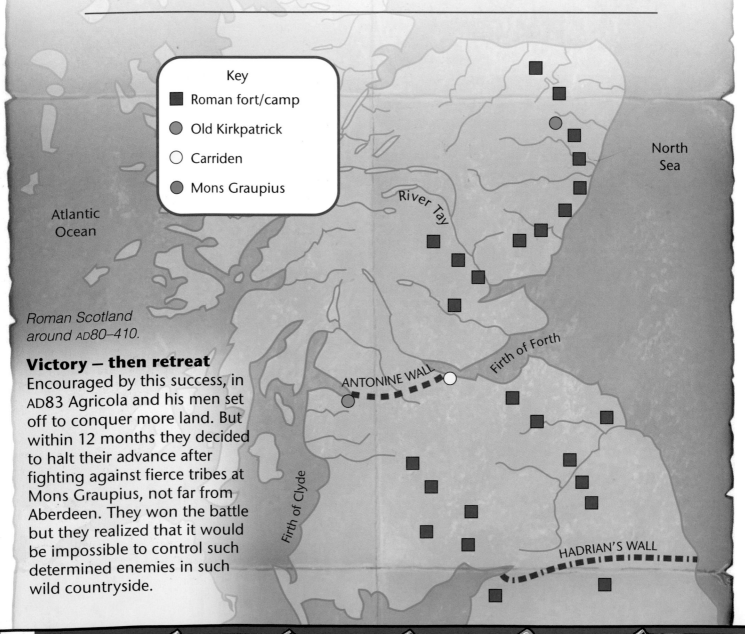

Key
■ Roman fort/camp
● Old Kirkpatrick
○ Carriden
● Mons Graupius

Atlantic
Ocean

River Tay

North
Sea

*Roman Scotland
around AD80–410.*

ANTONINE WALL

Firth of Forth

Firth of Clyde

HADRIAN'S WALL

Victory — then retreat
Encouraged by this success, in
AD83 Agricola and his men set
off to conquer more land. But
within 12 months they decided
to halt their advance after
fighting against fierce tribes at
Mons Graupius, not far from
Aberdeen. They won the battle
but they realized that it would
be impossible to control such
determined enemies in such
wild countryside.

Roman tombstone showing a Roman soldier spearing Celtic warriors.

Defending the frontier

To mark the limit of the land they controlled and keep out invaders from the north, the Romans built a huge frontier barrier – Hadrian's Wall. Work began in AD122. When finished, the Wall stretched right across Britain from east to west.

A second wall

In AD139 the Romans tried once again to invade land north of Hadrian's Wall. As before, they quickly occupied the lowlands region and in AD143 decided to build a second barrier, the Antonine Wall, to defend their newly won territory. But hostile tribes forced the Romans to retreat and they abandoned the Antonine Wall around AD160.

Peaceful contacts

Most people fought against Roman invaders. However, some lowland chiefs were friendly. Merchants from many parts of Scotland even traded with the Romans. And Roman farmers introduced new crops and animals to Scotland, including garlic, carrots, rabbits and domestic cats.

The Antonine Wall was 57 kilometres (35 miles) long, 3 metres (10 feet) high and 4.3 metres (14 feet) wide.

Did you know?
The Celtic chief, Calgacus, said that the Romans "...make a desert and call it peace". This is the first recorded comment by a "Scot".

The Roman Empire

AD81	AD84	AD122	AD143	AD367	AD410
Romans invade Scotland.	Romans defeat Celts at battle of Mons Graupius.	Romans begin to build Hadrian's Wall.	Romans begin to build Antonine Wall.	Tribes from Scotland and Ireland attack London.	End of Roman rule in British Isles.

The Painted People

When the Romans first arrived in Scotland they met many different groups of Celtic people living there. There were Selgovae, Votadini and Damnonii (in the Lowlands), and Decantae and Caledones (in the Highlands).

But who were all these different peoples? Mostly they were Celtic tribes – groups of families owing loyalty to a chosen chieftain who protected them and rewarded them if they served him faithfully. When the Romans first reached Scotland they came into contact with at least 12 separate tribes there. The Romans reported that the Caledones were the most hostile tribe; the Votadini were the most friendly.

Each Celtic tribe controlled its own territory and spoke its own local language.

"The Picts"

In AD297, a Roman writer called the people of northern Scotland a new name – the Picts (Painted People). In the past, historians put forward all kinds of theories about the Picts, claiming that they were foreign invaders, barbaric pre-Celtic peoples or a "lost tribe". Today, experts think that none of these theories is true.

This Pictish stone shows men hunting on horseback – a favourite Pictish pastime.

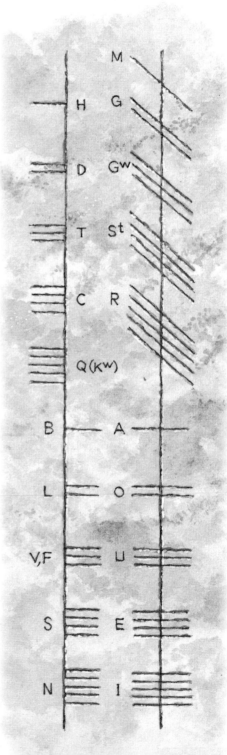

Some Pictish people were able to read and write. They used a system of lines called Ogham script to record messages on carved stones.

United tribes

Instead, most historians now believe that the Picts were simply the descendants of northern Celtic tribes, including the Caledones and the Decantae. Over the years these tribes had joined together. It helped them to fight more strongly against Roman invaders. By uniting different tribes, Pictish kings had built up a large kingdom in north and east Scotland.

Royal rule

Pictish kings were warriors who demanded loyalty, army service and farm produce from tribe members; in return they gave them land and weapons, and offered them protection. They stayed powerful until around AD900. Under their rule, a new Pictish culture developed.

Continuing traditions

This Pictish culture grew out of ancient Celtic traditions. For example, Pictish troops put on body paint before battle like earlier Celtic warriors. Pictish people spoke a Celtic language. (Scholars today call it "P-Celtic".) Pictish art was strongly influenced by swirling Celtic patterns, although Pictish artists also invented new designs based on symbols shaped like animals.

Scotland Divided

The Romans left the British Isles in AD410. For the next 400 years and more, Scotland was divided into many separate kingdoms. People living there spoke different languages, obeyed different laws, followed different leaders and were often at war.

North and east Scotland belonged to the Picts. The far west of Scotland (modern Argyll and the Inner Hebrides) was home to a different group of people, the Gaels. They called their kingdom Dal Riata and they had close links with tribes living in north-east Ireland.

Neighbours or invaders?
Some historians think that the Gaels migrated from Ireland to settle in Scotland; others think the Gaels and the Irish were simply close neighbours who shared the same culture.

Alt Clut (Dumbarton Rock, in west-central Scotland). The kings of Strathclyde ruled from a fortress here.

Did you know?
The people of Scotland did not call themselves "Scots". The Romans gave them that name – it meant "pirates".

Southern kingdoms

After around AD400 the Celtic tribes of lowland Scotland also set up their own kingdoms. The most powerful was Strathclyde, based in Dumbarton. Further south was Rheged, which stretched south into Cumbria. The land around Edinburgh belonged to the kingdom of Gododdin. The people of all these three kingdoms were known as Britons, and they spoke a Celtic language similar to Welsh.

A painting, from the "Book of Kells", decorated with Gaelic designs. It was painted in Dal Riata around AD780.

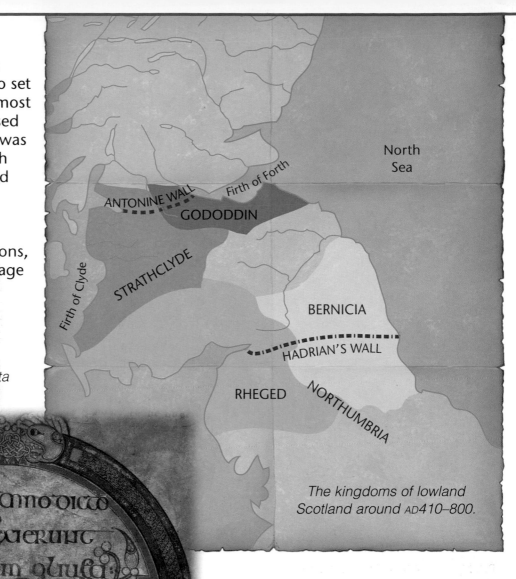

North Sea

ANTONINE WALL
Firth of Forth
GODODDIN
Firth of Clyde
STRATHCLYDE
BERNICIA
HADRIAN'S WALL
RHEGED
NORTHUMBRIA

The kingdoms of lowland Scotland around AD410–800.

Ruled from England

The far south-east of Scotland was part of the kingdom of Bernicia. This was ruled by the Angles – Germanic people who invaded eastern England soon after AD400. Its capital was at Bamburgh, in Northumbria.

In spite of their differences, people in all four Scottish kingdoms lived in much the same way. In fertile lowland areas, ordinary families worked on large estates belonging to the king or nobles. In the Highlands, they kept cattle and made butter and cheese. Around the coast, people went fishing.

Christianity Arrives

The early peoples of Scotland worshipped many different gods and goddesses. But after the Romans invaded, a new, very different religion reached Scotland – Christianity.

Christian beliefs were carried to lowland Scotland by Roman soldiers, traders and government officials. Friendly Celtic chiefs were probably the first people in Scotland to become Christians. They believed that Christianity was a newer and better way of worshipping God, but probably did not give up many of their earlier beliefs in spirits and magic.

Christian clues

It is not known when most Scottish people became Christians, but Christian burial sites and stones carved with Christian words have been found in southern Scotland dating from around AD450. Poems written around AD550 also describe Christian warriors from Strathclyde, Bernicia and the Pictish kingdom.

Missionaries

These early Christians were taught and guided by churchmen, some of whom were honoured as saints. Some saints, like Ninian (died around AD550) from Bernicia, worked as missionaries, travelling and preaching the Christian message.

The first Christians built monasteries in wild, lonely places so they could pray and study without interruptions.

This container for holy relics belonged to St Columba. After his death it was honoured as a lucky talisman and carried into battle by Scottish warriors.

Bishops...

Some saints, like Kentigern, bishop of Strathclyde (died around AD620), were organizers. They appointed priests to care for local communities and persuaded nobles to pay for churches. They also worked with kings – Christians needed strong defenders.

...and monks

Other saints, like Columba (died AD597), led communities of monks and nuns who devoted their lives to prayer. St Columba inspired the people he met so much that Scottish kings asked to be buried at his monastery on Iona.

Whose laws?

Over the years the Celtic Church in Scotland developed its own ways of worshipping. This led to differences with the Church led from Rome. In AD664 a special Synod (meeting) was held in Whitby, England. After much discussion, the Celtic Church eventually agreed to follow Rome's laws.

But there were also quarrels within the Celtic Church. By around AD700 church leaders had become rich and played a powerful part in politics. This angered a protest movement, the *Celi De* (Servants of God), who called on Christians to lead poor simple lives.

St Martin's cross, Iona, carved between AD700 and 800. Tall stone crosses were built to advertise places where people could listen to preachers.

Vikings made surprise raids on churches, monasteries and farming villages close to the coast.

Viking Raiders

In AD794 Irish monks reported that there was "a laying waste by the heathen of all the islands of Britain". The next year pirates plundered St Columba's monastery on the holy island of Iona. The Vikings had arrived!

The Vikings were raiders from Scandinavia who travelled across dangerous seas in sleek, fast "dragon ships". Most Vikings who attacked Scotland came from Norway. They were looking for excitement, adventure, new lands to settle and rich treasures to carry away.

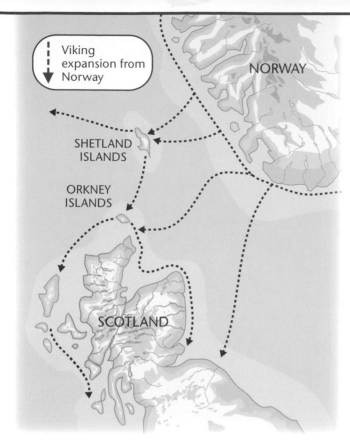

Between AD800 and 1100 Vikings settled throughout the north and west of Scotland.

Take-over!

Viking raiders recognized that Scotland would be a good place to live, and families of Viking farmers soon followed them. By around AD850 the Vikings had taken complete control of the Shetland and Orkney islands. In AD839 they conquered southern Pictish lands and in AD870–871 captured the capital of Strathclyde. By around AD1000 they ruled most of the land north of the Great Glen, all the western islands and all the western coast.

All the Scottish kingdoms now faced crisis. Some collapsed completely, others joined together to fight back.

Neighbours

Everywhere they settled in Scotland, Viking families lived alongside Pictish, Briton or Gaelic neighbours. In some areas like Galloway and Argyll this created a new, mixed culture known as "Gall-Gaell" (foreign Gael). But in Orkney, Shetland and the western islands, Viking settlers introduced their own language, technology, religious beliefs and artistic traditions to replace earlier Celtic ones.

Did you know?

Many treasures owned by Scottish kings, monks and churches disappeared in Viking times. Some were taken back to Scandinavia, others were hidden away.

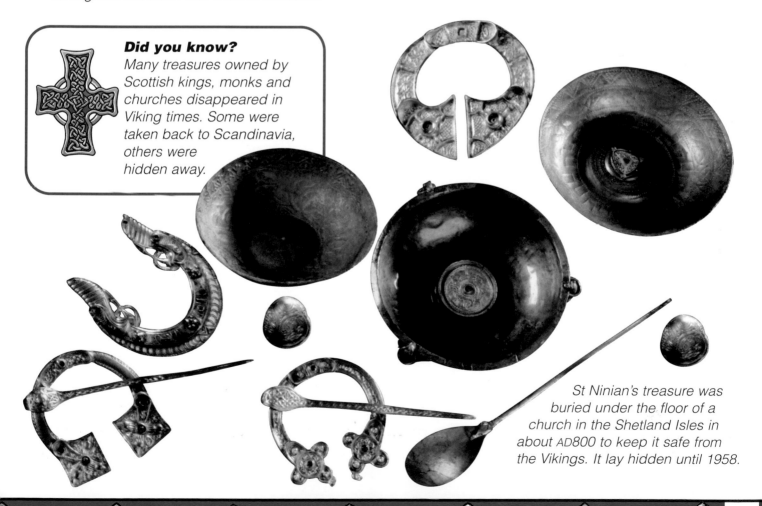

St Ninian's treasure was buried under the floor of a church in the Shetland Isles in about AD800 to keep it safe from the Vikings. It lay hidden until 1958.

Kings and Armies

After around AD800, years of fighting between warring kingdoms and Viking invaders, together with new Christian ideas, had brought many changes to Scotland.

Scotland's kings still lived in grand style. They built great halls to welcome their warriors and entertain them with lavish feasts. They chose trusted warriors as their companions and paid bards to commemorate their victories in songs and poems.

Royal records

But royal government had changed. Rulers now wanted their kingdoms to be better-controlled and more organized. Increasingly, kings relied on powerful nobles called "mormaers" (district governors) to help them rule. Mormaers summoned soldiers to fight in new royal armies, collected tributes (taxes) and kept law and order. Helped by trained scribes (usually priests) they also began – for the first time in Scotland – to keep written records of kings' reigns, soldiers, ships and royal finances.

Kings travelled around their kingdoms to win support from local nobles and impress ordinary people.

New local lords

Christianity called for less violent behaviour, new ways of worship and a new hope of heaven. But in most parts of Scotland, poor families still lived in the same way, farming and fishing. They bartered food and livestock for useful items made by local craftworkers. They still gave a share of their produce to their local overlord in return for his protection. But that lord might now be a Viking or even a monastery. After around AD800 Vikings and the Church controlled large areas of Scotland.

After receiving gifts of lands from kings and nobles, the Celtic Church became one of the most powerful landowners in Scotland, collecting rent (paid in produce) or demanding work from ordinary families.

Christian kings

Kings were still expected to be brave and war-like and to defend their kingdoms from outside attack. But now they also had to support the Church – which preached peace. In particular, church leaders tried to end bloody feuds between rivals claiming the right to the throne. But if a king ruled well he could rely on support from church leaders who told all Christians to obey him.

This carved stone shows a fight between the Picts and the Angles in AD685. The Picts won – the body of the Angles' dead king is being eaten by a raven at the bottom right of the stone.

Birth of a Nation

For thousands of years, Scotland was not a united nation. But between around AD800 and 1300, fearsome warriors and quarrelsome kings created the first Scottish nation. New ideas arrived from England – and Scotland faced a dangerous new threat from English kings.

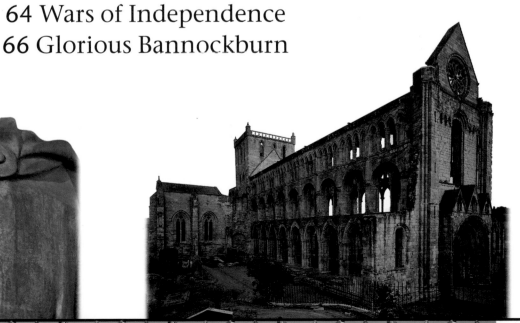

Creation of Alba

In 842 Kenneth MacAlpin, a warlord from Argyll in Dal Riata, western Scotland, took control of the Pictish kingdom as well as his own lands. For the first time, a large part of east and west Scotland was united under one ruler.

Kenneth won control of both kingdoms by fighting. In 839 many Pictish warriors were killed in battle by the Vikings. Kenneth saw that the Pictish kingdom was weak, and attacked. At least four other warlords challenged his right to rule Pictland. (At that time, all men descended from Pictish rulers could claim to be king.) But Kenneth overpowered them.

Kenneth moves his court

To mark the joining of Argyll and Pictland, Kenneth arranged a solemn, splendid ceremony in 849. He removed the remains of Argyll's favourite saint, Columba, from the western island of Iona to the village of Dunkeld, in the heart of Pictland. Kenneth also set up a new royal court at Dunkeld, and made it the centre of his united kingdom.

By moving St Columba's relics to his new kingdom, Kenneth hoped church leaders – and warriors – from Dal Riata would come to Pictish lands to help him stay in power.

This Pictish stone carving depicts warriors hunting on horseback.

A new nation

Kenneth died in 858. As well as creating a combined kingdom, he also founded a new ruling dynasty (family). His descendants ruled Pictland and Dal Riata until 1043.

By creating a new royal family and moving powerful Gaelic people to Pictish lands, Kenneth laid the foundations for a new nation. Slowly, Pictland and Dal Riata joined together. By 900 this combined kingdom had a new name – Alba.

Friends and enemies

Kenneth was the first to unite Pictland and Dal Riata, but for years there had been contact between Pictish and Gaelic rulers. Often, they fought bitterly. But sometimes they made alliances to fight against rival kingdoms in south Scotland, and against Viking invaders.

These walrus-ivory chess pieces portray fierce Viking invaders.

Did you know?

After Kenneth took control of his kingdom, Pictish people joined Dal Riata warriors to fight the Vikings. And they began to think of themselves as part of the new kingdom of Alba.

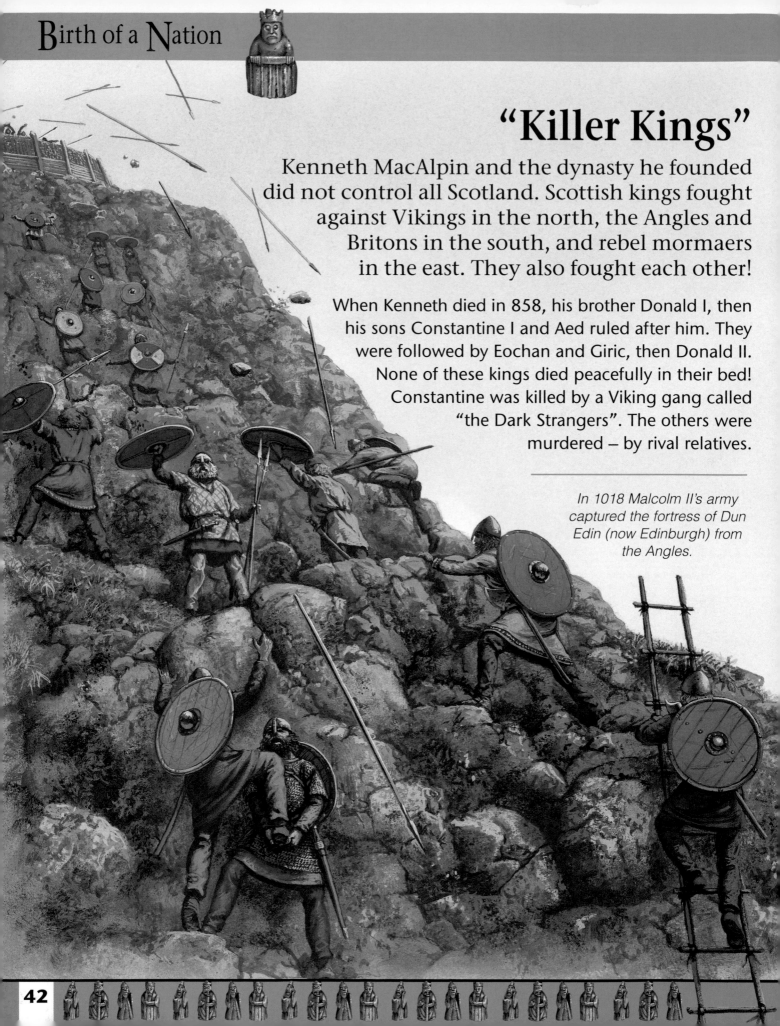

"Killer Kings"

Kenneth MacAlpin and the dynasty he founded did not control all Scotland. Scottish kings fought against Vikings in the north, the Angles and Britons in the south, and rebel mormaers in the east. They also fought each other!

When Kenneth died in 858, his brother Donald I, then his sons Constantine I and Aed ruled after him. They were followed by Eochan and Giric, then Donald II. None of these kings died peacefully in their bed! Constantine was killed by a Viking gang called "the Dark Strangers". The others were murdered – by rival relatives.

In 1018 Malcolm II's army captured the fortress of Dun Edin (now Edinburgh) from the Angles.

Staying alive

All these royal murders were very bad for the kingdom. So Constantine II, who became king in 900, worked out a plan to try and stay alive.

He made an agreement with his cousin (and chief rival) that members of the royal family should take it in turns to rule. He promised that his cousin's son, Malcolm, would be king after him – and survived safely for the next 40 years! He was the first ruler to be proclaimed "King of Alba".

By touching the Stone of Scone — also called the Stone of Destiny — early Scottish kings showed their devotion to their kingdom.

More murders

As agreed, Malcolm I became king and named Constantine's son Indulf as his heir. But Malcolm was killed fighting the Angles in 954. Indulf also fought the Angles, capturing their fortress at Edinburgh before dying in battle in 962. But then the system of kingship by turns broke down and none of the next five kings lived long or died peacefully. They were: Dubh (962–967), Culen (967–971), Kenneth II (971–995), Constantine III (995-997) and Kenneth III (997–1005).

Alba grows

After these five unhappy reigns, the next king, Malcolm II, kept hold of power from 1005 to 1034. He was a very successful warrior, defeating the Angles in 1018 and the Britons in 1020, and won new land in southern Scotland. When he died, Alba was a larger, richer kingdom.

Malcolm II's grandson, Duncan, became king after him but was killed by Macbeth, Mormaer of Moray, as shown in this 19th-century painting by George Cattermole. Macbeth ruled from 1040 to 1057 and was killed by Duncan's son!

Malcolm and Margaret

Malcolm III Canmore ("Big-chief") became king of Alba in 1058. He was the son of Duncan and his army had killed Macbeth. But as a man and as a ruler he was not like either of them.

Malcolm became friends with the English king, Edward the Confessor. He learned to speak English as well as his native Gaelic, met English nobles and church leaders, and found out about English customs and laws. He found out about these when sheltering in England, while Macbeth ruled Alba.

Viking friends

Malcolm also made friends with the Viking warlords who had conquered Anglian lands, and married a woman from a Viking royal family. When the time came for him to claim the Scottish throne, his Viking allies helped him fight against Macbeth. In return, he gave them land in southern and eastern Scotland.

A scene from the Bayeux Tapestry, showing William the Conqueror's knights defeating English soldiers, 1066. Malcolm Canmore supported the English who rebelled against the conquerors.

Viking words

These new Viking landlords brought Viking words and Viking customs with them, which had a lasting impact. They stopped Gaelic and Pictish culture from the west of Scotland spreading further south. Viking words blended with Briton and Anglian ones to create a new language, Lowland Scots.

Daring raids

So that he could rule more efficiently, Malcolm set up a new capital at Dunfermline. It was much further south than the old Alba capital, Dunkeld, and near the centre of the kingdom. This now stretched from south of Hadrian's Wall to north of Inverness.

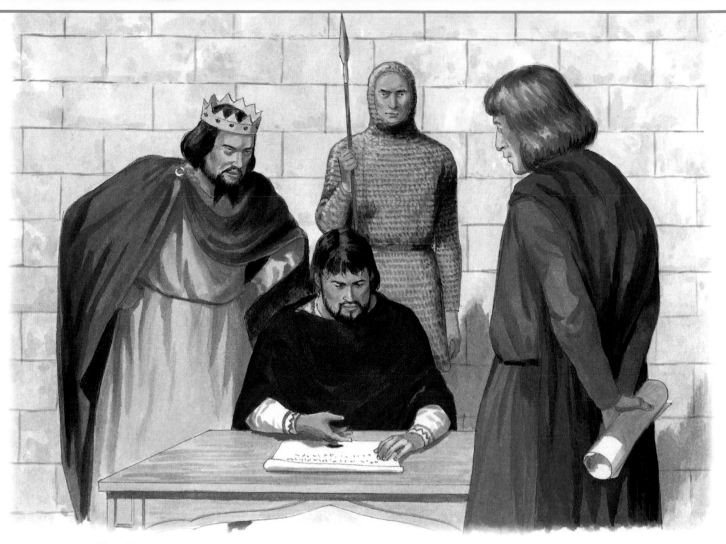

The English made Malcolm promise loyalty to William the Conqueror as Scotland's overlord.

Dangerous allies...

Malcolm also became involved in English politics by sheltering the English prince, Edgar. Edgar had led English nobles to rebel against William the Conqueror, who conquered England in 1066. To punish Malcolm, William invaded Scotland in 1072 and forced him to accept a truce.

...and a new wife

Edgar's stay in Scotland had another, surprising result. He brought his mother and sisters with him. By now, Malcolm's Viking wife had died so he decided to marry Edgar's sister, Margaret.

Did you know?

Malcolm's promise to William the Conqueror was very dangerous. It gave English kings the right to claim Scotland as their own land.

Malcolm's wife, Margaret, pictured in a 19th-century stained-glass window.

Church and State

Queen Margaret, wife of Malcolm III Canmore, was one of the most remarkable women of her time. She brought many changes to Scottish life and was made a saint after her death.

Margaret was the daughter of an English prince and a Hungarian princess. She had seen much more of the world than her husband – she spent her childhood in Hungary – and could speak several languages. By marrying Margaret, Malcolm was linking Scotland with powerful ruling families all across Europe.

For the first time in Scotland, Margaret made all the royal children learn to read and write.

Gifts to the Church

Margaret was a deeply religious woman. Like earlier Scottish rulers, she gave money to the *Celi De* (Celtic religious communities) and to churches founded by Gaelic and Pictish kings. She also set up a new river crossing (Queensferry, near Edinburgh) to help pilgrims travelling to St Andrews, the chief religious centre in former Pictish lands.

Queen Margaret's new ferry encouraged more pilgrims to visit the holy city of St Andrews.

"Civilizing" Scotland

To make Scotland (and its royal family) more "civilized", Margaret introduced new rules for anyone attending the royal court. They had to be clean, well dressed, polite and preferably of noble birth. And she gave all her sons and daughters English, not Celtic, names so everyone would remember their proud English heritage.

New religious ideas

Margaret also paid for new church buildings. She persuaded Scottish bishops to reform the way church services were held and to get rid of ancient Celtic religious customs. Margaret's generosity to the Church brought great prestige to Scotland.

Margaret paid for a splendid church in the capital city, Dunfermline, and a monastery housing a community of English monks.

Viking Scotland

For over 500 years, from around 900 to 1469, Scottish kings did not rule all Scotland. The far north of the Scottish mainland, the Orkney and Shetland isles and the Hebrides (islands off Scotland's west coast) were ruled by Viking earls and warriors, and by kings of Norway who were their overlords.

Viking settlers and local people (Picts, Gaels and Britons) developed their own special way of life. They built longhouses in Viking style with rooms for people at one end and animals at the other. They used Viking words, followed Viking customs, obeyed Viking rulers and followed Viking laws.

A new frontier

Scottish kings did not like foreign rulers controlling Scottish land, and fought to win it back. Their first success came in 1098 when King Edgar of Scotland forced Norwegian king Magnus Barelegs to retreat to a new frontier – all the land he could sail around. This left Magnus as overlord of the Scottish islands but Scottish kings now ruled the mainland.

Alexander's demands

Next, in the 1240s, Alexander II of Scotland ordered King Hakon of Norway to give up all the Scottish islands. Hakon refused and in 1263 sent a huge fleet of 40 ships to Scotland. The Scots defeated them in a sea battle at Largs.

Traders from Iceland, Scandinavia and many Scottish islands met at markets in Viking Scotland.

Ruins of the large Viking settlement at Jarlshof, in the Shetland Isles. It contained farmhouses, byres (cattle-sheds) and store-rooms.

The end of Norway's power

In 1266, the new Norwegian king, Magnus the Lawgiver, gave all the western islands to Scotland in return for a large sum of money. Norway continued to rule Orkney and Shetland until 1469, but then they too were returned to Scotland as part of a marriage agreement between the Scottish king, James III, and a Norwegian princess.

Viking Power

around 900	around 980	1035	1098	1156	1263
Viking earls (lords) conquer Orkney and Shetland.	Viking kingdom on Isle of Man controls Hebrides.	Viking Thorfinn the Mighty conquers land in north-mainland Scotland.	Magnus Barelegs retreats from mainland Scotland but keeps Scottish islands.	Half-Gaelic, half-Viking Somerled wins control of south Hebrides from King of Man.	Battle of Largs. Scots defeat King Hakon and Scots rule Hebrides from 1266.

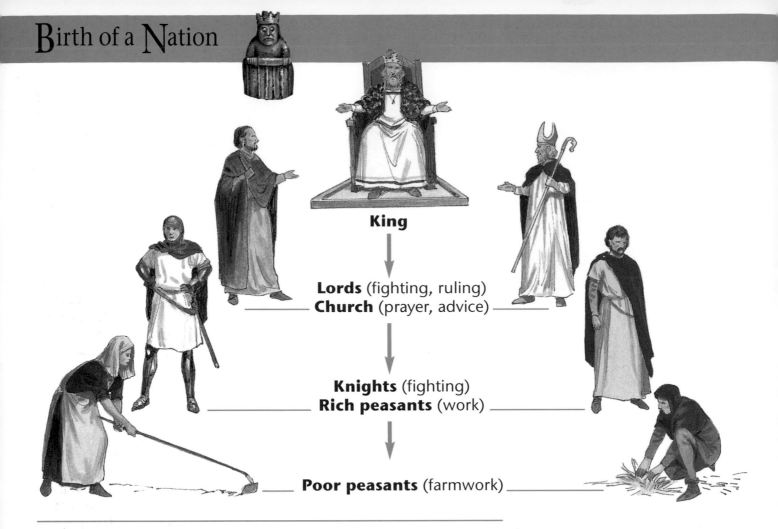

King

Lords (fighting, ruling)
Church (prayer, advice)

Knights (fighting)
Rich peasants (work)

Poor peasants (farmwork)

English Ideas

When Malcolm and Margaret died in 1093, they left four sons – Edmund, Edgar, Alexander and David. Malcolm also had a son, Duncan, from his first marriage. Malcolm's brother, Donald Ban, was still alive as well.

For four years, the whole kingdom was in confusion as to which of them should rule. Backed by many Scottish nobles, Donald Ban seized power. He wanted to abolish the changes Margaret had made and return to old Scottish ways. But Duncan invaded with an English army and forced Donald to fight. Edgar helped Donald defeat Duncan and they divided the kingdom between them. Then, in 1097, Edgar attacked, helped by more English soldiers, and reigned peacefully until 1107, when his younger brother, Alexander I, became king.

King David I introduced English "feudal" ideas to Scotland. Everyone, from lords to peasants, had to work in return for occupying land.

A successful career
Meanwhile David, the youngest brother, became a trusted companion of the English king, Henry II. He watched and learned how Henry made royal government stronger. He also married a wealthy English noblewoman, whose family once owned large estates close to Hadrian's Wall.

David returns

Before Alexander died in 1124, he named David as his heir. But David still had to fight rebel nobles in Moray to secure his place on the throne. Once there, he introduced many of Henry II's new ideas to prevent any further rebellions or old-fashioned family feuds.

Royal charters, such as the example above, which dates from around 1127, were issued by King David I of Scotland. They gave rights and privileges to the new churches and monasteries he founded.

Tough government

David made Scottish nobles promise not to rebel, and built royal forts close to their land to make sure they kept their promises. He founded new towns where royal officials could collect taxes, and new churches and monasteries, staffed by priests who would support royal rule. He copied Edgar's idea of keeping careful written records of all royal orders – so there could be no quarrels over them in future.

In England and Scotland, peasants worked hard on estates (large areas of land) belonging to kings, lords and the Church. This calendar illustration, dating from between 1310 and 1320, shows men harvesting wheat with reaping hooks.

Knights and Castles

David I worked out yet another way to keep his kingdom under control. He invited men he could trust from England to settle in Scotland, and gave them homes and land in return.

The men David chose were knights – expert fighting men. Like the kings and lords who ruled England, they were mostly part-English and part-French. Their ancestors had arrived in England with William the Conqueror and had married English noblewomen. At first they had French names but these soon became Scottish – for example, "de Brus" turned into "Bruce".

No choice

Once in Scotland, these Norman knights were obliged to serve King David and his grandson, Malcolm IV. They had few friends in Scotland, apart from the kings, and many Scottish lords distrusted them.

David's new knights built castles to defend their land, and to provide comfortable living quarters for their families, soldiers and servants.

Fighting on horseback

David's new knights had much better weapons, armour and horses than many Scottish lords, and were well trained in the latest ways of fighting. Using their superior weapons, the knights charged ranks of foot-soldiers, making them run for their lives.

Splendid strongholds

To protect themselves from attack by rebels fighting the king, or by Scottish people who resented their power, the new knights built splendid castles – the first of their kind in Scotland.

Where possible, these castles were built on naturally well-defended sites, such as islands or rocky crags. If not, workmen created a motte (artificial earth mound). On top of this they built an inner keep (tower) with private quarters for the knight's family, as well as a large hall where he could feast and where his soldiers and servants slept on the floor. The keep was surrounded by an outer bailey (castle yard) that housed kitchens and workshops.

A Scottish knight on horseback, pictured on the royal seal of King Alexander I.

Did you know?
Knights had to help the king govern, lead his army and provide fighting men whenever Scotland went to war.

Bothwell Castle, in the Central Lowlands of Scotland, was built soon after 1300 for the Douglas family in the latest French style. Its great stone tower took 36 years to complete.

Monks and Bishops

David I followed the example set by his parents, Malcolm and Margaret, and his brother, Alexander I. He encouraged religious reform. Like them, he realized that a strong Church would bring glory to Scotland and help the royal family stay in power.

Scotland had an ancient Christian tradition. By King David's time (1124–1153), there were already monasteries at old holy sites, such as Iona, Whithorn and Dunkeld. There were also religious men and women called *Celi De* (Servants of God) who lived in small communities.

Monks strolled in the cloisters (covered walkways surrounding the monastery garden) to take exercise, meditate (think deeply) and discuss spiritual problems with their community.

The ruins of Jedburgh Abbey, in the Scottish borders region. It was founded around 1118 by the future king, David I.

Working for God

In most monasteries, monks worked in fields and gardens to grow their own food. Some were herbalists and doctors, some were scholars who wrote books, and many were craftsmen. They designed religious buildings, painted stained-glass windows and copied out manuscripts – beautiful hand-written books with decorated pages.

Monasteries had libraries and "scriptoria" – special rooms where monks made copies of holy books.

New reforms

Many of these rules – like allowing Celi De to be married – seemed shocking to church leaders elsewhere in Europe. They thought that the Scottish Church needed reform, and the royal family agreed. Alexander, then David, arranged for new bishops (senior churchmen) to be appointed. It was their task to make sure priests performed their duties and all Christians followed the latest teachings of the Catholic Church.

These reforms led to quarrels with church leaders in England, who claimed the right to control Scottish Church life. So David appealed to the Pope (head of the Catholic Church). An answer finally came in 1192. The Pope declared that he would govern Scotland himself, from Rome.

How monks lived

David also invited church leaders from Europe to set up new monasteries in Scotland. They introduced strict new rules to tell monks how to live. Some monks (called Cistercians) were expected to lead tough lives of hard work, prayer and solitude. Others (called Cluniacs) were supposed to spend one-third of their day in prayer, one-third working and one-third resting – and to get up at night several times for church services.

Towns, Trade and Industry

For centuries, Scotland was different from most of Europe.
It was all countryside! The first real towns were not built
in Scotland until around 1150.

These first towns, known as "burghs", included Perth, Aberdeen, Edinburgh,
Inverness and Glasgow. (Later, they grew into Scotland's most famous cities.)
They were founded by kings, great nobles or monasteries, as trading centres.
Some towns had special privileges, such as the right to trade overseas.
Most had their own special laws.

*Each town also had a market-place
where people sold fresh foods and
country produce.*

Town design

These new Scottish towns were based on European ideas. Their streets of wooden houses were often laid out in a European-style grid pattern. They were all protected by strong gates and wooden walls. Beyond the walls, there were fields, vegetable gardens and grazing land for animals. Many towns were guarded by a castle and most had a stone-built church. Almost all had a harbour where cargo ships could unload.

The Edinburgh seal. Each town council had its own seal, which was fixed to documents to show they were genuine.

Who lived in towns?

Town-dwellers were divided into several groups. The most important were burgesses – wealthy merchants who often ran the burgh community as mayors and councillors. The burgh council was also responsible for collecting taxes on goods that were traded, and for arranging to sweep the streets and punish thieves.

A large number of burgh-dwellers were craftsmen and women, trained in tailoring, jewellery-making, weaving, making candles from wax or tallow, and sewing gloves and shoes. Others worked as butchers, bakers or fishmongers, sailors, boat-builders and dock-hands, or as builders and carpenters.

Town poor

As towns grew, many poor landless people moved there looking for work. Some became servants or labourers. A few lucky ones trained for a skilled career. But many lived in crowded, unhealthy lodgings and had to beg and scrounge to survive.

> **Did you know?**
> There were no Scottish coins until the reign of David I (1124–1153). Scottish traders had to use Roman, Viking or English ones, instead!

Town blacksmiths, depicted in this 14th-century manuscript illustration, made knives, swords, locks, latches, horse shoes, buckles and cooking pots.

Scottish raiders rode south across the border to attack English estates and drive away their cattle.

Border Wars

For many centuries, the kingdom of Scotland included lands south of Hadrian's Wall. The countryside there was wild and used mostly for grazing cattle. But politically, it was very important – it was the cause of the wars between Scotland and England.

There were two reasons for this. Powerful English families owned estates there and wanted to stop Scots raiders. The land also marked the border between rival English and Scots kingdoms. They fought to decide: were English kings the overlords of Scottish ones? Should Scottish kings pay them homage (make promises to obey)? Was Scotland independent, or just part of England?

Paying to be free

Malcolm's brother, William I, won the land back but tensions continued. In 1174 William was captured by English troops. To get out of prison he promised to pay homage to Henry II for all his Scottish lands. But when Henry II died and Richard I became king of England (who wanted money to fight in the Crusades), William was set free in return for a huge fine. The Scots were independent again!

No superior!

After William died, his grandson Alexander II (ruled 1214–1249) continued to invade northern England and to protest Scotland's independence. But he died suddenly, leaving a 7-year-old son, Alexander III, as king. Once again, England saw a chance to meddle in Scottish politics. Henry III arranged a marriage between his daughter and Alexander III. But, young as he was, Alexander III refused to do homage to Henry.

King Henry II of England, shown here in a chronicle from the 13th century, ruled from 1154 to 1189. He drove the Scots out of northern England.

England interferes

England was bigger and richer than Scotland, so English kings felt able to meddle in Scottish politics. For example, in 1160 Henry II of England helped Malcolm IV of Scotland (ruled 1153–1165) put down a rebellion in Galloway, and took control of northern England from the Scots.

While King Alexander III was still a child, and too young to take part in politics, rival nobles argued about how to govern his kingdom.

England and Scotland 1073–1244

1073	1092	1138	1139	1174	1244
England's William the Conqueror invades. Malcolm III does homage to him.	William II of England takes Cumbria; builds Carlisle castle.	Battle of the Standard – England defeats Scots.	David I of Scotland reconquers northern England.	English capture Scots king William I; he accepts English overlordship (released from this 1189).	Peace treaty with England.

In the Highlands, farmers grew crops in fields close to their houses and grazed cattle on mountain pastures.

Highlands and Lowlands

In different parts of Scotland, people lived in very different ways. Their lives were shaped by ancient customs passed down by their ancestors, and by their environment. The biggest difference was between Highland and Lowland life.

Did you know?
Scottish people even spoke different languages. In the north, they spoke Norse (Viking), in the west Gaelic, in the central Lowlands Scots, and in the far south-east English.

In the Lowlands, where there were river valleys, rolling hills and fertile soils, most people worked on great estates owned by kings, lords or monks. They built villages of straw-thatched houses with walls of wood and wattle-and-daub. Most villages were clustered around a green (communal open space) with a stone church nearby. Villagers raised sheep, pigs and cattle, and used horses and oxen to pull carts and ploughs. They planted wheat, oats, rye, barley, peas, flax and hemp.

Farm industries
Some villagers set up workshops to make pottery and iron tools, built watermills to grind grain, and mined small quantities of coal, silver and lead. Men tanned animal skins to make leather. Women spun wool into thread and wove it into cloth.

Highland life

In the Highlands, there were rocky mountains, deep sea lochs and very little fertile soil. Villagers here built houses with turf walls and roofs thatched with heather, and dug fields with a foot plough to grow oats, flax and barley. They raised black, long-haired cattle and garrons (ponies), caught fish from the sea and lochs, and gathered seaweed.

Highland cattle had thick shaggy coats to withstand harsh mountain weather.

Women's tasks

Highland farmers divided all the village land into three: inbye (the best land near the village); outbye (poorer land further away); and rough grazing land, high on mountain slopes. Women led cattle to the grazing land in springtime, and lived there all summer in rough shelters called shielings.

Clans and chiefs

In return for their land, highland families paid rent to clan chiefs who lived in castles, or to "tacksmen" (wealthy landowners). They relied on chiefs for protection and to settle disputes; in return, chiefs expected Highlanders to fight for them in war.

Highland farmers cut brick-shaped slabs of peat to dry, then burn as fuel.

Who Should Be King?

Alexander III reigned, successfully, for almost 40 years. He defeated the Norwegians, controlled quarrelsome Scottish lords, made peace with England and encouraged trade. But he failed to provide his kingdom with a suitable heir.

Alexander had a wife and three children but they all died before him. So, when Alexander himself died in 1286 – after falling from his horse while hurrying to see his new, second wife – his only heir was his granddaughter. She was known as "the Maid of Norway" – her mother was one of Alexander's daughters and her father was the Norwegian king. She was just 3 years old.

The voyage from Norway to Scotland was too cold and rough for the young Maid of Norway to endure.

A dangerous decision

By asking King Edward I for help, the Guardians had made a very unwise decision. They had encouraged England to be Scotland's overlord. Edward summoned Balliol to appear in English law courts, and demanded that Scottish nobles join the English army. Balliol refused and in 1295 signed a new treaty with England's enemy, France.

This 13th-century illustration shows King Edward I of England (right) sitting with his court. He was a famous warrior – with ambitions to conquer Scotland.

Too young

The Maid was too young to rule, so a council of six "Guardians" (lords and bishops) took over the government. They invited the Maid to Scotland and accepted King Edward I of England's plan that she should marry his son. But the Maid never reached Scotland. She died in Orkney in 1290.

Rivals

There was now no clear heir to the throne. Instead, 13 rival nobles claimed the right to be king. To avoid fighting among the rivals, the Guardians asked Edward I of England to help. He suggested that Scottish noble John Balliol, Lord of Galloway, should rule. Balliol was declared king in 1292. Balliol worked hard to restore law and order, appointing new sheriffs and calling meetings of the Scottish parliament. He also encouraged international trade, especially with France.

(left) In this 18th-century painting by Benjamin West, King Alexander III was saved from the fury of a stag whilst hunting.

Wars of Independence

Edward I of England was furious about the Scottish alliance with France. In 1296, he sent an army to attack the Scots and soon defeated them at the battle of Dunbar. English knights captured John Balliol, stripped him of his royal robes and sent him to London as a prisoner. Once again, Scotland had no king.

Some Scottish nobles did not support Balliol's war with England. They were mostly descendants of Anglo-Norman knights who had come to settle in Scotland. They had lands and family connections in England and, in 1296, they agreed to pay homage to Edward when he declared himself the new king of Scotland.

After Balliol was stripped of his royal robes, he became known as "Toom Tabard" (empty coat).

At Stirling Bridge, the Scots massacred English soldiers as they advanced. The main English army was trapped helplessly behind dead bodies on the bridge.

England's enemies

But there were many Scots who refused to accept English rule. They included priests and bishops, minor gentry and a few great lords. They all joined together to fight Edward, and were led by Andrew Murray (from a powerful noble family in north-east Scotland) and William Wallace (the son of a Lowlands landowner).

Wallace wins

Wallace and Murray soon won control of all Scotland north of the River Tay, then marched south. In 1297, they defeated the English army at Stirling Bridge.

Quickly, Edward I sent a large new army and defeated Wallace at Falkirk the next year. Wallace survived but had to hide for years in the forests, making "hit and run" raids on the English.

Did you know?
At Stirling Bridge, the English Lord Treasurer, Hugh de Cressingham, was killed by the Scots. Then his skin was removed and cut into little bits, which were carried away by Scottish soldiers as souvenirs.

Wallace's brave fight to defend Scotland and his cruel death made him a Scottish national hero. This bronze statue of Wallace was erected at Edinburgh Castle in 1929.

The Hammer of the Scots

Worse was to come. In 1303 England and France made peace. Edward I invaded Scotland, captured the most important castles and forced Scottish nobles to pay homage to him. His determination to crush Scottish opposition gave him the nickname – "the Hammer of the Scots". Wallace was betrayed, captured, sent to England and brutally executed in 1305.

At Bannockburn, English knights and their horses became hopelessly trapped in boggy ground.

Glorious Bannockburn

By 1306 Edward I was in control of the Scottish kingdom. John Balliol was still in prison and English armies occupied most Scottish castles. But Wallace's brave fight – and grisly death – inspired other Scots to keep on fighting.

The new leader of Scottish fighters was Robert Bruce. Descended from an Anglo-Norman family, he was the greatest lord in Lowland Scotland. At first he had supported the English against Wallace but, when he saw he had a chance to become the Scottish king, he changed sides. In 1306 Bruce was crowned Robert I.

Forced to flee

The new king lost no time in recruiting an army and forced all Scottish lords to swear loyalty. But the English sent an army to kill him and Bruce was forced to flee. Bruce fought on against the English for the next eight years. His determination and success at recapturing castles attracted many Scots to join his fight.

A famous victory

Edward I of England died in 1307 and the new English king, Edward II, was much less war-like. Even so, faced with growing support for Bruce, he invaded Scotland in 1310–1311 and again in 1314. The Scots and English armies met at Bannockburn near Stirling. Against all odds, the Scots won a famous victory which preserved their country's independence for the next 400 years.

In 1320 Scottish nobles wrote to the Pope: "… it is liberty alone we fight for… which no honest man will lose, unless he dies". Later, their letter was known as "the Declaration of Arbroath".

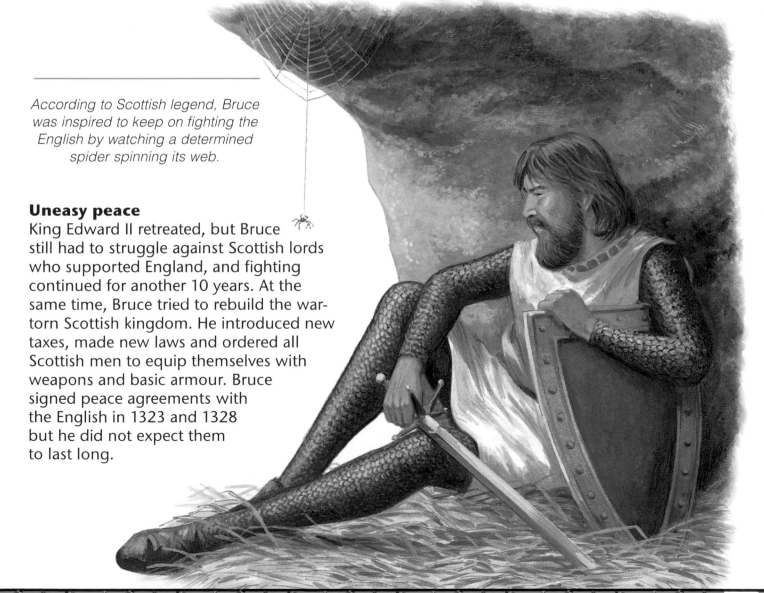

According to Scottish legend, Bruce was inspired to keep on fighting the English by watching a determined spider spinning its web.

Uneasy peace

King Edward II retreated, but Bruce still had to struggle against Scottish lords who supported England, and fighting continued for another 10 years. At the same time, Bruce tried to rebuild the war-torn Scottish kingdom. He introduced new taxes, made new laws and ordered all Scottish men to equip themselves with weapons and basic armour. Bruce signed peace agreements with the English in 1323 and 1328 but he did not expect them to last long.

Stewart Scotland

Between 1300 and 1600 Scotland was transformed. It changed from a weak country claimed by rival warlords into a confident nation ruled by energetic, intelligent kings – and one fascinating, foolish queen.

Fight for Survival

King Robert the Bruce died in 1329. The next king, David II, was Bruce's son but he was only five years old. He spent the rest of his life struggling to defend his kingdom and to stay in power.

David was threatened by three groups of enemies. The first were ambitious Scottish nobles, who were appointed as guardians to rule Scotland while David was a child. They included members of the powerful Douglas family.

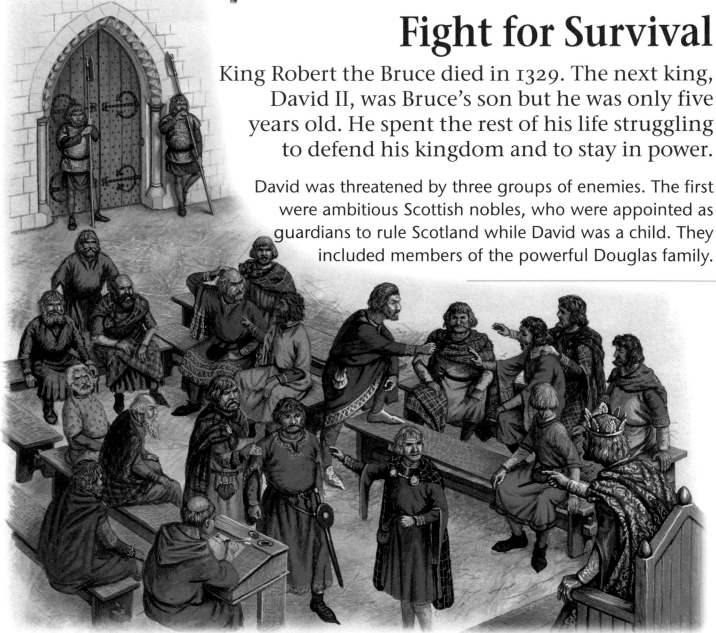

From the reign of David II onwards, members of the Scottish parliaments demanded the right to be consulted about planned new taxes.

English attacks

The second threat to David II came from Edward Balliol, son of John Balliol, who had been made king of Scotland in 1292. Now Edward was demanding the right to be king. He was backed by some Scottish nobles who hoped to share in his power. Balliol was also helped by the third threat to David's rule – the English king, Edward III. He hoped to take control of David's kingdom by claiming to be Balliol's overlord, and sent an army north to attack in 1333.

Did you know?

David II was married at four years old! His bride, Joan, was seven, and the sister of the English king, Edward III. The marriage was an attempt to secure peace with England.

Parliament becomes powerful

The English finally agreed to release David on payment of a huge ransom. To find the money for this the Scots had to raise taxes, especially from towns. So that town leaders would agree to these new taxes they were summoned to meetings of the Scottish Parliament.

From 1357 these meetings of Parliament became regular and marked a big change in Scottish politics. Town citizens had become full members of the political community and played a part in discussing government policy.

After around 1300, there were more towns in Scotland. They grew richer, and more powerful in politics.

This coin shows David II proudly controlling a spirited war-horse. He wanted people to think he could govern Scotland as easily.

Years in prison

The next year, David (now aged 10) was sent to France for safety. While he was abroad, Robert the Steward (his cousin and nearest heir) led the fight against Edward III.

David returned in 1341, and in 1346 led an invasion of England. But he was captured and spent the next 11 years in an English prison. While he was there, Robert the Steward took charge of Scotland. David was so desperate to escape that he considered naming Edward III as his heir. But Robert the Steward would not agree.

Scottish Parliaments

before 1290	**July 1290**	**1326**	**1357**	**1366**
Kings meet nobles and churchmen at "colloquia" (official meetings). Laws made and taxes agreed.	The name "Parliament" first used for colloquia meetings. Same members and duties as before.	Representatives from royal burghs (towns founded by kings) called to Scottish Parliament.	Representatives from towns join churchmen and nobles as regular Scottish Parliament members.	Scottish Parliament tries to stop royal actions such as taking food for the royal court without paying for it.

New Rulers

King David II died in 1371, leaving no children. His closest heir was his nephew, Robert the Steward, who became Robert II. He founded a new dynasty (ruling family) – the Stewarts, or Stuarts – who ruled Scotland for the next 300 years.

By medieval standards, Robert was an old man (55) when he came to the throne, but he had many years of government experience. He was also extremely rich, and used this money to control the government and win friends among the nobles. He wanted them to support him and help him rebuild war-torn Scotland.

Royal marriages
Robert II also made useful friends by marrying his daughters to rich Scottish families, and his sons to European princesses. These European weddings were designed to make the Stewart family seem more royal and more powerful.

Douglas danger
In 1390 Robert II died. The last years of his reign were troubled by plots among nobles, especially the Douglas family, trying to seize power.

The Douglas family controlled the borderlands between Scotland and England. Other nobles, related to the Stewart family, held top government positions and controlled vast estates in the north-east. One noble, Alexander Stewart, known as "the Wolf of Badenoch", terrorized the countryside with his own private army.

In 1390 Alexander Stewart, the "Wolf of Badenoch", attacked the town of Elgin, looting its treasures and burning its cathedral to the ground.

Robert III

Plots against royal power continued after Robert II's sickly son, John, became king. He took the name "Robert III". Like his father, Robert III could not control his kingdom. In the Highlands, nobles fought private wars and, in 1396, 60 warriors from two rival clans met at Perth and fought to the death. King Robert's brother, the Duke of Albany, kidnapped Robert's oldest son and shut him up in prison where he died. Most people said that Albany had starved him to death.

Robert III, shown on this silver groat (coin), knew he was a failure as a king. He asked to be buried in a dunghill when he died.

Kidnapped!

For safety, Robert then decided to send his only other son, James, to France. But James's ship was captured by pirates, who handed him over to the king of England. The news of this killed Robert III, who died in 1406, leaving Albany in power.

Doune Castle, near Stirling in central Scotland, was built by the powerful Albany family soon after 1400.

New Problems

The next Scottish king, James I, spent the first 18 years of his reign (1406–1437) as a prisoner in England. Albany ruled Scotland until he died in 1420. Then, Albany's son, Murdoch, took over, but not for long.

In 1424 the English government agreed to release James – if the Scots paid another ransom. James had learned much in England. He knew all the latest dances and was skilled at many sports. He had also seen how strong English kings, such as Henry IV and Henry V, ruled. He arrived in Scotland with new ideas to "reform" his kingdom.

James I (ruled 1406–1437) brought new English ideas to Scottish government.

Linlithgow Palace, rebuilt by James I in 1424.

Ending Albany power

First of all, James was determined to remove the Albany family from power and to keep all other nobles under control. He executed the most important Albany men, and seized Albany lands for himself. James then took back the right to collect customs tolls from noble families, and used the money to fund an elegant royal lifestyle and build a splendid new palace at Linlithgow.

James also took steps to control religious life in Scotland, burning heretics and quarrelling with the Pope.

"Civilized" behaviour

But James still had to find the money to pay his ransom. He tried to persuade the Scottish Parliament to raise taxes but its members refused – partly because they feared he would spend the money on luxuries for the royal family. Parliament did agree, however, to let James make new laws to "civilize" ordinary people's behaviour. These included stopping late-night drinking and banning football.

Old-fashioned enemies

James's tough government brought peace to Scotland but also made him many enemies. After he led a failed attack on the English in the borderlands, they decided to get rid of him. He was killed by a group of nobles in 1437.

One brave lady-in-waiting tried to bar the door with her arm as James I's enemies attacked the royal lodgings at Perth. They soon overpowered her.

Did you know?
James I died in a sewer! He climbed into the drains to escape his attackers, but they caught him and stabbed him to death.

The Unlucky Kings

Like many Scottish kings before him, James II came to the throne (in 1437) when he was a child, aged six. He only just managed to survive his childhood years when rival governors of royal castles plotted to kidnap him and seize power.

James II also had to fight against the ambitious Douglas family. In 1440 he invited the Earl of Douglas to dinner at Edinburgh Castle. Douglas was then dragged out of the castle and beheaded!

Twelve years later, James invited the next Douglas earl to his castle. When Douglas refused to end his alliance with James's enemies, James killed him! After this, all Douglas lands were taken by Scottish kings.

In 1452 James II stabbed the 8th Earl of Douglas to death in Stirling Castle.

Killed by a cannon

The Stewart royal family were now richer and more powerful than any other Scottish family. But bad luck lay ahead ... James was a keen soldier and wanted the latest weapons for his troops. In 1460, aged only 30, he was killed by one of his own new cannons when it exploded.

Nicknamed "Mons Meg", this 15th-century cannon, now in Edinburgh, is similar to the weapon that killed James II.

A quarrelsome king

The reign of his son, James III, was also unfortunate. James III continued the Stewart tradition of trying to increase royal power. He chose priests and clerks to be his ministers. This angered the nobles, who feared they were being kept out of the government. He increased taxes and interfered with law courts. He also quarrelled with his younger brothers and had them tried for witchcraft!

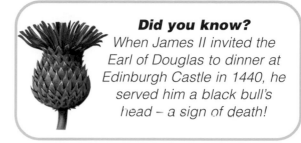

Did you know?
When James II invited the Earl of Douglas to dinner at Edinburgh Castle in 1440, he served him a black bull's head – a sign of death!

Wet and weary, James III sheltered in a mill after losing the battle of Sauchieburn in 1488. That night a mysterious stranger arrived – and murdered him!

Success ... then murder!

Outside his own lands, James was at first more successful. His ministers won back Orkney and Shetland for Scotland, and James himself ended the power of the Lords of the Isles.

But then, to the dismay of most Scots people, James made friends with the English king. Outraged nobles rebelled against him in 1482, capturing his chief supporters and hanging them. In 1488, James was defeated in battle by more Scottish enemies, then mysteriously murdered – probably by his own teenage son.

Lords of the Isles

James I's strong government overpowered many Scottish ruling families, except the MacDonalds. They were descended from Somerled, a half-Viking, half-Gaelic warlord who died in 1164. By James's time, they ruled a large area in north-west Scotland, and since 1336 they had called themselves "Lords of the Isles".

The MacDonald lords had no legal right to this title. They claimed it because of their strength. They were supported by clans of Highlanders, led by local chiefs. These chiefs came to the MacDonald headquarters on Islay to decide on policy towards "foreign" powers, such as England and the rest of Scotland. Clan chiefs also commanded their own armies of clansmen, and recruited "gallowglasses" (soldiers from Ireland, who fought for pay) for extra support.

Old-fashioned rulers

James I, and the kings who followed him, thought the Lords of the Isles were old fashioned. They spoke Gaelic and relied on the ancient clan-system for their power. But they were also dangerous to the new, united nation the Stewart kings were trying to create. The Stewarts fought several battles against the Lords of the Isles but neither side won a clear-cut victory.

The Lords of the Isles left behind many relics, such as this warrior gravestone at Finlaggan, Islay.

The end of an era

Then, in 1462, the Lord of the Isles (John II) signed a treaty with the Stewart kings' two great enemies – the king of England and the head of the Douglas family – to divide all of Scotland between them.

King James III was furious and demanded that the Lord of the Isles obey him. James made him live as a royal "guest" in the east-coast city of Dundee, far from John II's power-base in western Scotland. Finally, in 1493, King James IV took over all the Lord of the Isles' lands.

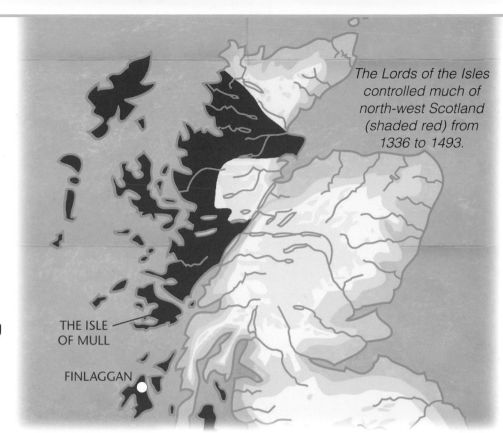

The Lords of the Isles controlled much of north-west Scotland (shaded red) from 1336 to 1493.

THE ISLE OF MULL

FINLAGGAN

The battle of Bloody Bay, off Mull, 1481, where the King's fleet clashed with the Lords of the Isles.

Troubled Times

While kings, nobles and clan chiefs were fighting, ordinary men and women worked hard to make a living. In the countryside, they kept cattle, grew oats and barley, and gathered wild foods. In towns, they ran market stalls or craft workshops. Around the coast they worked on fishing boats or in the import–export trade.

Some country people, like "tacksmen" (wealthy farmers), rented large farms and employed poor "cottar" (landless) families. They were rich enough to afford large homes, good meals and warm clothing. Families of merchants and skilled craftworkers also led a comfortable existence in towns. But all Scottish people faced a new danger in 1349.

Burying dead bodies during the Black Death, as imagined by a 19th-century artist.

The Black Death

That year, plague arrived in Scotland. It was a deadly disease carried by rats and fleas, which spread very quickly through crowded villages and towns. The first outbreak (called the "Black Death" by later historians) killed around one-third of all Scottish people in just two years. There were further outbreaks at regular intervals for the next three centuries.

Better for workers

Plague caused terrible grief and shock. But its huge death-toll brought some benefits to the survivors. After 1350 workers were in short supply so lords could no longer force "neyfs" (unfree men and women) to live on their estates and labour for them. Other ordinary workers could also bargain for better pay and conditions. And, as workers' wages rose, prices fell because traders had fewer customers left alive to sell to.

Woollen cloth, sold in Scottish towns, was made by women workers at home. They cleaned and combed sheep's wool, spun it into thread and wove it by hand on looms.

Hungry and homeless

At first, these high wages and low prices led to a boom in trade – especially for wool and leather – and to new prosperity for towns. But repeated attacks of plague, the high cost of wars, high taxes to pay for royal ransoms, and the poor quality of Scotland's coinage all caused economic crisis before too long. By 1450 the price of food had trebled. Poor people now faced hunger and homelessness, as well as disease.

Scottish merchants sailed north to trade with Scandinavia and Baltic lands. This 16th-century engraving shows the busy harbour at Stockholm, Sweden, around 1500.

Did you know?
Medieval coins were made of silver. In the 15th-century economic crisis, Scottish governments mixed silver with copper to save money. But people did not trust this money, and prices rose higher.

Fishermen, Pirates and Explorers

Scotland is almost completely surrounded by sea. And before roads were built, or cars, trains and planes were invented, the quickest way to reach most places was to travel by boat. Scottish people developed many sea-based industries, especially fishing, salt-making and carrying goods by cargo ship.

Scottish fishermen caught hundreds of tonnes of salmon and herring. A few fish were taken ashore and sold to be eaten fresh, but many more were salted then packed in barrels. Preserved like this, they would stay edible for months and could be stored to eat in winter or transported inland.

North-European trade

Scottish expertise in sea travel made it easier for Scots merchants to trade with European countries to the north and east, across the stormy North Sea, than to travel overland to southern England. Scottish ships sailed to Denmark, Germany, the Netherlands and states around the Baltic Sea, carrying cargoes of cattle hides, sheepskins, wool, salted fish and coarse woollen cloth.

Fishermen in small boats, called cobbles, used nets to catch salmon in river estuaries around the Scottish coast.

Attacking the Hanse

Scottish sailors also tried to get rich by attacking other ships, especially heavily laden cargo vessels belonging to the Hanseatic League – a group of very wealthy trading cities in northern Europe.

Hanse ships carried valuable luxury goods, such as Scandinavian amber, German glass and metalwork, and Russian furs. By 1412, the problem of Scottish piracy had grown so bad that the League halted all trade with Scotland as a punishment.

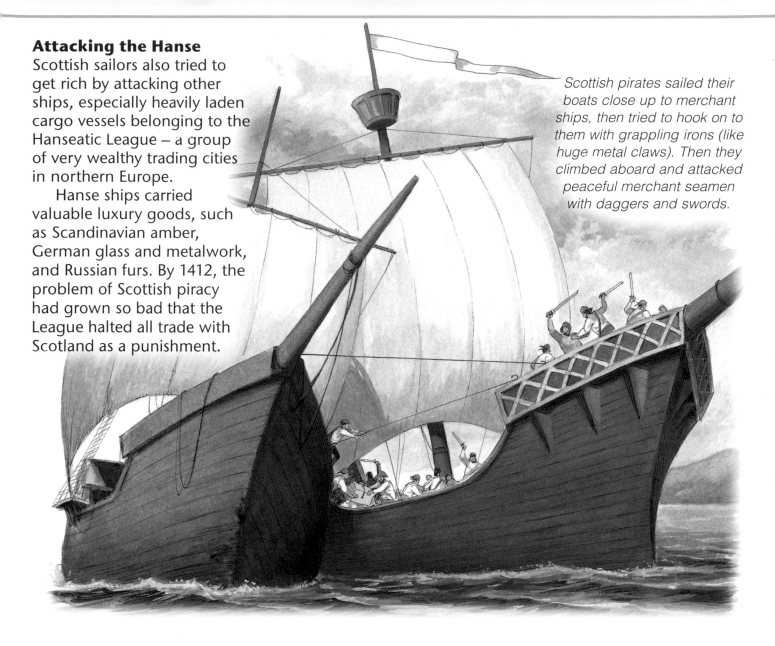

Scottish pirates sailed their boats close up to merchant ships, then tried to hook on to them with grappling irons (like huge metal claws). Then they climbed aboard and attacked peaceful merchant seamen with daggers and swords.

Pirates and kings

Kings of England also made complaints about attacks on English merchant shipping. To fight this piracy, many Scottish trading towns tried to ban the sale of goods captured in raids at sea. But they failed because Scottish kings, especially James IV, secretly encouraged pirate attacks as a way of annoying his enemies in England.

Scottish fishermen faced competition from large ships, called "busses", that sailed from the Netherlands to catch fish in the North Atlantic Ocean.

Schools and Universities

Until around 1600 most Scottish people could not read and write. There were only about 100 schools in the whole of Scotland, and just three universities.

A schoolmaster and his pupils around 1600.

Most schools were run by the Church and were attached to cathedrals and monasteries. There, boys learned "grammar": how to read and write in Scots and Latin.

Nunneries ran similar schools for girls, and towns such as Perth and Aberdeen set up grammar schools for the citizens' children. There were also song schools, where pupils learned church music.

Trained to work

In theory, church schools and town schools were open to all, but in practice, only children from wealthy families could attend. Poorer parents could not afford the fees. They sent their children to train as apprentices, and to learn useful skills by helping local merchants and craftsmen, or made them work around the house or on the farm.

Did you know?
In 1595, the boys of Edinburgh High School rebelled – and shot their teacher!

New universities

The first university in Scotland was founded at St Andrews in 1412. It was followed by universities at Glasgow (from 1451) and Aberdeen (from 1495). All three were set up by the Church, and staffed by church scholars. Their purpose was to train young men to be priests, teachers or lawyers. Students learned theology (the study of religion), church law and national law, Hebrew and ancient Greek (the languages of the Christian holy book, the Bible) and philosophy (the study of thinking). These first universities were very small – St Andrews had around 100 students in 1500.

Scots schoolboys played football, golf and shinty – a rough, wild kind of hockey.

After around 1500, printed books spread new information and new ideas. This is the first Scottish printer's mark, created by Andrew Myllar in 1506.

No more religious schools

After the Reformation, the Church in Scotland became Protestant. Some university teachers were dismissed and others left to live in Catholic countries in Europe. New, Protestant teachers – mostly ministers – took their place. In 1579, song schools were also taken away from church control and were run by town councils.

James IV's new palace – Holyrood House, Edinburgh.

"Good King James"

King James IV inherited the throne in 1488 but did not rule independently until 1495. He felt guilty about killing his father, James III, and wore an iron belt for 40 days each year to show he was sorry. But that did not stop him from being one of Scotland's most successful kings.

In 1495, James IV was young (only 22) and fascinated by the latest scientific ideas. He experimented with medicine by paying volunteers to let him practise dentistry. He mixed strange alchemical potions, trying to create gold. He encouraged a French inventor, Jean Damian, to make a test flight from the top of Stirling Castle. It failed – but Damian survived. He spent large sums to re-equip the navy, and his new warship, the *Great Michael*, launched in 1511, was the finest of its time.

Renaissance style

James was very keen on the latest "Renaissance" styles in art and architecture. He used them to help build a fine new palace at Holyrood, close to Edinburgh. The new "modern" style impressed people, and showed the Stewart dynasty in a good light .

Meeting the people

James liked meeting ordinary people and listening to their problems. He reformed the law and made long journeys to hear important court cases and settle local feuds. He raised money by taxing the Church and rich nobles, and by renting out some royal estates, rather than by making demands in Parliament.

Peace ... then war

In 1503 James married Margaret Tudor, daughter of the English king, Henry VII. It was a political marriage, arranged as part of a peace treaty agreed between Henry and James to try and end the costly wars between their kingdoms. But sadly this peace did not last. When a new king, Henry VIII, inherited the English throne, fighting began again. James, and most of the top Scottish noblemen, were killed at the battle of Flodden in 1513.

At the battle of Flodden in 1513, James IV ordered his soldiers to charge too soon. They were shot to pieces by English archers.

James IV (ruled 1495–1513) was intelligent, artistic and famous for many romances.

James IV and New Ideas

1496	1500	1501	1505	1507	1510	1511
New laws encourage education.	Top musicians and poets serve at the King's court.	Holyrood Palace, Edinburgh, built in latest style.	College of Surgeons founded in Edinburgh.	First printing press in Scotland.	Jean Damian experiments with flight at Stirling Castle.	Warship *Great Michael* launched.

The Auld Alliance

James IV died leaving only one lawful heir – a son, James V, who was 17 months old in 1513. At first, James V's great-uncle, the Duke of Albany, ran Scotland, then the Douglas family took control. James escaped from their control in a daring midnight ride in 1528 when he was just 16. He led an army to Edinburgh and forced all other nobles to swear obedience to him.

James V (ruled 1513–1542), portrayed on a carved wooden roundel from the ceiling of Presence Chamber, Stirling Castle.

James faced two big problems – how to control proud lords and border raiders, and how to defend Scotland against English Henry VIII, who aimed to prove himself Europe's greatest king. James V locked up the nobles and hanged the most dangerous raiders. He founded a new court of justice and spent lavishly to improve the royal family's prestige. He built palaces at Falkland and Stirling, and ordered fine gold coins (bearing his portrait) and a magnificent new crown.

James V's splendid new palace at Falkland, built in the latest French style.

United against England

To help fight off the threat from England, James decided to strengthen the "Auld Alliance". This friendship between Scotland and France had been important since medieval times. Now, James joined France in supporting the Catholic Church, which was being criticized by religious reformers. This displeased English Henry VIII, who was quarrelling with the Pope over his divorce.

Mary Queen of Scots

James V's only surviving child was a daughter, Mary. When he died, she became Queen of Scots at just one week old. Her French mother, Mary of Guise, took control of the government and imported French courtiers and troops to help her rule. When young Mary was six her mother sent her to France for safety and arranged her marriage to the French crown prince.

Mary Queen of Scots was betrothed to the French crown prince at the age of six.

Defeat, disgrace and death

James annoyed Henry still further when he chose two French noblewomen to be his wives. His first wife, Madeleine, died in 1537 soon after reaching Scotland; James then married Mary of Guise the next year. By 1542, Scotland and England were at war. At first the Scots were victorious but, after his troops lost the battle of Solway Moss in 1542, James collapsed, fell ill and died.

Did you know?
Like his father, James V liked talking to ordinary people and listening to their problems. But he chose to do this in disguise, dressed up as a peasant.

Reforming Religion

From the time of St Margaret, Scottish people had followed the Catholic Church, led by the Pope in Rome. They went to Mass (the most solemn church service), prayed to God and the saints, and gave money for holy statues and family memorials. They also paid the Church to forgive their sins and guarantee their souls a place in heaven.

The Catholic Church was remote from most people (its services were in Latin, not Scots or English), and bad practices had spread among its clergy. Because of this, by around 1520, religious reformers known as "Protestants" began to call for new ways of worshipping. They wanted churches to be plain and simple, priests to live pure, holy lives, and services to be held in local languages so that everyone could understand them. They wanted the Bible (the Christian holy book) to be translated from Latin so that people could read it.

This 19th-century stained-glass window in St Giles' Cathedral, Edinburgh, shows Protestant leader John Knox preaching.

The ruins of Sweetheart Abbey. Protestant reformers attacked churches and other buildings belonging to Roman Catholic monks.

Protesting voices

In Scotland, calls for reform were led by George Wishart and John Knox. The Scottish government, headed by Catholic Mary of Guise, saw them both as a threat. In 1546 Wishart was burned as a heretic (false believer). The next year Knox was exiled but he did not stop writing or preaching. In 1558 he published *The First Blast of the Trumpet against the Monstrous Regimen of Women* – a book strongly criticizing female rulers, such as Mary.

A new Scottish Church

In 1560 Knox encouraged nobles and townsmen meeting at the Scottish "Reformation Parliament" to ban the Catholic faith, and set up a new, Protestant, national church. This was to be governed by a National Assembly of believers, and organized according to a "Book of Discipline" drawn up by Knox himself.

Many Scottish Protestants were burned to death for refusing to give up their religious beliefs.

Reformers wanted the new Scottish Church to be run on Presbyterian lines. There were to be no bishops, monks or priests. Instead, each group of Protestants should choose its own minister for his scholarly knowledge of the Bible and God-fearing way of life.

Mary Queen of Scots, portrayed in 1578. She was beautiful, wilful and foolish.

Mary Queen of Scots

Mary Queen of Scots returned from France in 1561. She was 18 years old and a widow – her husband, the young, sickly King of France, had died. Her mother was also dead and so it was now Mary's duty to rule, alone.

But Mary knew little about her kingdom. She had spent most of her life in France, spoke French and liked the elegant lifestyle of the French court. She had no experience of governing – and she was a Catholic.

A foolish marriage

Just two weeks after reaching Scotland, Mary was faced by angry Protestant demonstrations led by John Knox. She agreed to keep her own faith private, and to appoint both Catholic and Protestant nobles to her new government.

But in 1565, she angered them all by choosing to marry a foolish, ambitious, half-English teenager, Henry Stuart, Lord Darnley. No Scots wanted him as their king. Mary's own half-brother led a rebellion against her but it failed.

Murder at court

Mary brought French culture and fashions to the Scottish court. Many Scots admired these, but Mary's court was soon rocked by scandal. In 1566 her Italian secretary, David Rizzio, was murdered as he clung to her for protection. Mary, who was pregnant, was unharmed. A few weeks later, she gave birth to a son.

Did you know?

It was rumoured that Mary was in love with a rough, tough, Scottish nobleman called Bothwell. She supposedly asked him to kill Darnley, her feeble English husband, so that they could run away together.

Mary fled to England, hoping that her cousin, Queen Elizabeth, would help her win back the Scottish throne. But Elizabeth put her back in prison.

A new love

Darnley was suspected of plotting to kill Rizzio, but was himself murdered the next year. This time the prime suspect was James Hepburn, earl of Bothwell – a Scottish nobleman. Europe was outraged when Mary ran away with Bothwell and married him. Furious Scottish Protestant nobles locked Mary up in Loch Leven and forced her to abdicate (resign as queen).

But Mary still had some supporters. In 1568 they helped her escape to England. There, her cousin, Queen Elizabeth I, was appalled at the way Mary had been made to give up her throne. But she also feared that Mary might encourage English Catholics to rebel. So she put Mary in prison to remain captive for the next 19 years.

Loch Leven Castle, Tayside, where Mary was imprisoned by Scottish nobles from 1567 to 1568.

Rebellious Subjects

James VI – the son of Mary Queen of Scots and Henry Darnley – was crowned king in 1567, aged 13 months. He never knew his parents but he grew up to be a respected and successful king.

While James was young, Scotland was ruled by governors called regents. They struggled to stop the country being torn apart by civil wars. Fighting began in 1571 between the "King's Lords" (mostly Protestants, loyal to James) and the "Queen's Lords" (mostly Catholics, loyal to Mary).

Young King James VI of Scotland (later James I of England), painted around 1585 when he was 19 years old.

In 1582, in the "Ruthven Raid", a gang of Scottish nobles ambushed King James VI while he was out hunting, and tried to kidnap him.

James takes control

James finally forced the rival lords to end their fighting in 1585, and took swift action to stop them ever trying to control the government again. He passed new laws, strengthening royal officials and removing nobles from royal councils. In 1594 some lords protested but their rebellion was soon put down.

Ending Highland wars

James also made plans to end other quarrels throughout Scotland. Clans in the Highlands region were still taking part in bloody feuds, mostly over land. This lawless behaviour was terrorizing the countryside. In 1587 James made new laws against rebellion. These were followed in 1598 by orders to all Scots to settle quarrels in law courts, not by fighting.

There was also lawlessness among ordinary people. Bad weather and poor harvests meant that many were homeless, hungry and unemployed. They could only survive by begging, and some had become bandits and thieves. James passed harsh laws giving town councils the right to whip beggars.

Catholic and Protestant

The most difficult problem facing James was continued quarrelling between Catholics and Protestants. He supported Protestants for political reasons. But James was also keen to make sure that all Churches obeyed royal orders, and wanted them to have bishops to lead them. In 1596 there were riots in Edinburgh when extreme Protestants disagreed.

In 1577, 390 members of the MacDonald family were trapped in a cave on the west-coast island of Eigg, and suffocated to death by MacLeod warriors during a war between rival clans.

The Crowns Unite

For the first 20 years of James VI's reign, his mother, Mary Queen of Scots, was still alive. She became the focus for plots against her cousin, Elizabeth I of England, by Catholics who hoped to make Mary queen. By 1587 Elizabeth felt that Mary had become too dangerous and had her executed.

Elizabeth was childless and, after Mary died, James VI became Elizabeth's heir. She did not like him but James knew that, one day, he would follow her as ruler of England.

Queen Elizabeth I of England ruled from 1558 to 1603. Strong and wise, she dedicated her life to her people.

In 1587, captive Mary Queen of Scots was executed on the orders of Elizabeth I.

United monarchies

Thoughts of this exciting future shaped the way James ran Scotland. England was Protestant and he knew that English people would not accept a Catholic king or a Catholic Church. So he supported Protestants in his kingdom in a moderate way.

When Queen Elizabeth I died in 1603, James VI of Scotland became James I of England as well. This united the English and Scottish monarchies, but the two kingdoms remained separate. Each still had its own parliament, government, language and laws.

In 1603, James VI of Scotland and I of England paraded through the streets of London, to meet the people of his new kingdom.

Did you know?
After he became king of England, James arranged for the body of Mary Queen of Scots to be moved to a place of honour in Westminster Abbey, London.

Peace at last?

James left Scotland in 1603 to live in England but he kept in close touch with Scottish affairs – it took just five days for messengers to ride on horses between Scotland and London. James's rich, new kingdom of England helped him to achieve his ambition to end wars between Scottish nobles. Using English money, he could now afford to appoint new – and loyal – officials to govern Scotland instead of relying on rival lords.

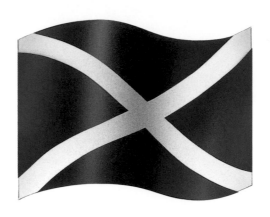

North Britain

In 1603 King James VI of Scotland inherited
the English crown. In 1707 Scotland and England
were united. How did these changes alter Scottish life?
And why did Scotland's capital city, Edinburgh,
become famous all round the world?

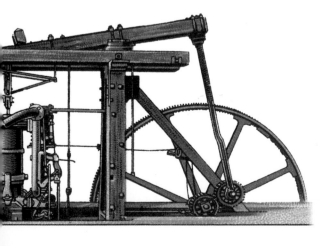

"The Wisest Fool"

From 1603 James VI of Scotland was known by two titles. His English subjects called him James I. They also laughed at his new nickname: "the wisest fool in Christendom".

James sometimes looked ridiculous – he was famously scruffy and grubby, which was not how people expected to see their king. His private life was also rather unusual. He made close friendships with a number of handsome young men (although he also had seven children with his wife, Princess Anne of Denmark). But James was not a foolish king. Overall, he ruled Scotland and England wisely and well.

Scottish emigration to Ireland

HEBRIDES

SCOTLAND

IRELAND
Belfast

ENGLAND

Irish Sea

James VI and I ruled Scotland from 1567 to 1625, and England from 1603 to 1625.

James VI sent Protestants from Scotland to settle in northern Ireland. He hoped they would support the English rulers of Ireland against Irish Catholics.

Failed aims
However, James did not succeed in achieving his main aims for his two countries. These were: to join Scotland and England in one United Kingdom; to interfere in the running of the Scottish Protestant Church; and to change the way English and Scottish people thought about their kings.

Divine Right

After James moved to England in 1603, he set up a commission (group of powerful people) to make plans for uniting his two kingdoms. But this scheme was thrown out by the English Parliament in 1607. Powerful people in England and Scotland also failed to agree with James's belief in the "Divine Right of Kings" – the idea that kings were appointed by God and therefore did not have to explain their actions to their subjects.

There was a violent thunderstorm when the Five Articles of Perth were agreed in 1618. Many Scots saw this as a bad omen.

New church laws

James faced even stronger opposition from the Scottish Parliament when he tried to make members accept new laws, changing the way Protestants worshipped. (James wanted to bring back old ceremonies and give bishops more powers.) Parliament refused, so James called a General Assembly of religious leaders. He threatened them with serious penalties if they did not agree, and so his new church laws, known as the "Five Articles of Perth", were passed. But many Scots refused to obey them.

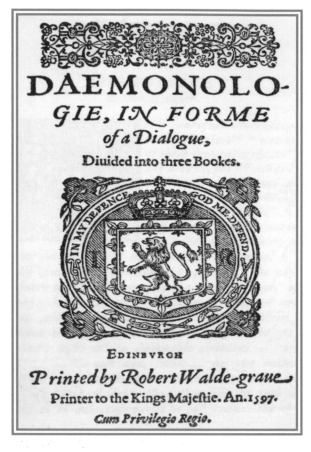

The title page of "Daemonologie", James VI's book about witchcraft.

Witch Hunts

Like many other people of his time, James VI was fascinated by witchcraft. He was intrigued by its magic and mystery but shocked by its spiritual danger. As a young man he made a study of witchcraft, which he published in a book called *Daemonologie* in 1597.

Witchcraft was a serious subject. In earlier centuries, church leaders thought that people claiming to be witches had fairly harmless magical powers. But from around 1500, ideas about witchcraft changed. Protestant ministers throughout Europe taught that witchcraft was wicked and that witches had made a pact with the devil.

Killing witches

Church leaders and rulers like James VI thought that witches were a threat to society and should therefore be killed. In 1563, for the first time in Scotland, witchcraft became a crime. Between 1550 and 1650 around 1,500 supposed witches were executed in Scotland and a further 2,000 were put on trial.

Threats and curses

Almost all people accused of witchcraft were women. They were usually old and poor. Some of them were traditional healers but most were just disadvantaged people who used threats of spells or curses to try to get what they wanted, or to settle quarrels with their neighbours.

Their accusers were often Protestant ministers, keen to enforce "godly discipline" among local communities and to end superstition of all kinds.

In 1590, witches at North Berwick, in the Borders region, were accused of making cattle sick, setting fire to churches and plotting against King James VI and I.

In the 16th and 17th centuries, almost everyone believed in magic and witchcraft. So it was easy to accuse unpopular people of bringing bad luck or casting spells.

Forced confessions

Witch-finders examined suspects for marks they said were signs of the devil, or deprived them of sleep for many days and nights so that their minds became disturbed. Then they confessed to non-existent crimes.

Witch-hunting became less common after around 1650 when new, more scientific ways of looking at the world began, and when Protestant communities became less fearful of people with alternative ideas. The last witch was executed in Scotland in 1727.

Covenanters

James VI died in 1625. He was followed as king of Scotland (and England) by his son, Charles I. Like his father, Charles believed in the Divine Right of Kings.

Charles I was born in Scotland but he moved to London with his father in 1603. After that he visited Scotland only twice: first in 1633, when he came to be crowned king. To the Scots he seemed very English! Charles tried to force them to accept English-style bishops to lead their national church as well as a new English prayer book. Since the Reformation Parliament of 1560, Scottish Protestant leaders had wanted their Church to be organized in a "Presbyterian" way, with church congregations choosing their own ministers. They did not want bishops, nor English prayers!

Charles I of England and Scotland was a devoted family man, but he made many mistakes as king.

The Covenant
In 1638 some leading Scottish Protestants drew up a National Covenant (Petition). It combined support for the Scottish Church with complaints about how Scotland was being treated by Charles's government. Many Scots saw Charles's ideas about religion – and his high-handed way of ruling – as "works of the devil". They believed it was their duty to battle against them so they organized local "Covenanting" armies.

This copy of the 1638 Covenant has survived until the present day.

Civil war

Fighting began in 1639 and at first the Covenanting troops were victorious. In 1641 Charles visited Scotland a second time, to ask for peace. But he also had enemies in the English Parliament and among Catholics in Ireland. They soon joined in the fighting and Britain now faced civil war.

Charles I surrendered to Scots soldiers at Newark-on-Trent in 1646.

Victory ... then defeat

Charles did have some friends in Scotland. They included nobles like the Marquis of Montrose. His troops – mostly Irishmen and Highlanders – defeated Covenanting armies in 1644–1645. But south of the border, Charles was less successful. He was taken prisoner by Scots soldiers in 1646, and handed over to the English Parliament in 1647 when the Scots army returned home.

Did you know?

In 1638 several copies of the Covenant were printed and sent to different parts of Scotland to be signed by supporters. Many Scots people were so keen to do this that they wrote their signatures using their own blood!

The execution of Charles I in London, as imagined by an 18th-century artist.

Cromwell's Commonwealth

After Charles I was captured in 1646 he offered to do a deal with the Scots. He would let them be Presbyterians if they would support him as king. But leaders of the Scots Covenanting armies would not all agree and Charles's Scottish supporters, who marched into England, were defeated by English army commander Oliver Cromwell in 1648.

As a result, Charles stayed a prisoner in England. In 1648 he was put on trial and in 1649 he was beheaded. Charles I's son, Charles II, now claimed the Scottish and English thrones. Many Scots supported him — mostly because they were angry with the English for not consulting them about the execution of Charles I. In Edinburgh, Scotland's capital, they proclaimed Charles II as the new king — so long as he let them remain Presbyterian.

In 1650, English Puritan leader Oliver Cromwell inflicted a crushing defeat on Scots Covenanters at the battle of Dunbar.

English victories

This infuriated the English who invaded Scotland in 1650. Once again English troops were led by Oliver Cromwell and he soon defeated the Scottish armies. Meanwhile, Charles II sought refuge in Scotland, and was crowned in a traditional ceremony at Scone. But in 1651 Cromwell's troops won another crushing victory against the Scots, and Charles II had to escape to France.

Keeping control

Cromwell used his victories to try to bring Scotland firmly under English control and make it part of the "Commonwealth" of Britain. He sent many Scots who had supported Charles I and Charles II into exile. With his trusted deputy, General Monck, he built forts from which garrisons of English soldiers could control the Scottish countryside. He also gave orders for Scottish MPs to attend Parliament in England.

In 1652 General Monck demanded the "Honours of Scotland" – a royal crown, sword and sceptre that were symbols of Scottish independence. But they were smuggled away by a Scottish Presbyterian minister's wife and her servants.

Royal Restoration

Oliver Cromwell ran Scotland with a Council of State and a permanent army. No nobles played a part in his government. This brought peace until Cromwell died in 1658. Two years later, Charles II returned from France to be king.

Charles did not like Scotland nor Presbyterians. He appointed a Scottish noble, the Earl of Lauderdale, to rule Scotland for him, and passed laws to bring back bishops to the Scottish Church. His supporters executed leading Scottish Presbyterians and imposed crippling fines on 800 others.

Conventicles

This angered many Presbyterian believers. They refused to go to church and organized secret prayer meetings, called "Conventicles", in wild, lonely places. Charles's Scottish ministers sent soldiers to track down Conventicles and punish anyone who attended them. This led to so many bloody fights that the years from 1684 to 1688 became known as "the Killing Time".

However, some Scots welcomed Charles II's royal rule. They included members of old noble families and Roman Catholics who shared his dislike of Presbyterianism.

Preaching to Presbyterians at a secret Conventicle meeting could be dangerous – or even deadly.

Did you know?
Many people said that baby James Edward was not Queen Mary's son. They claimed that he was smuggled into the royal bedroom (in a warming pan!) because King James was desperate to produce a male, Catholic heir.

During his reign, Charles II created mistrust and dislike of his rule among the majority of Scots.

James VII and II

Charles II died in 1685. He was succeeded by his brother, James VII of Scotland (James II of England), who was openly Roman Catholic. This was unpopular in many parts of Scotland (and England). In 1688 James's wife, Queen Mary, gave birth to a son, James Edward, and had him baptized as a Catholic. The following year, a group of powerful Scottish politicians declared James had lost his right to rule. The English Parliament also told him to go. By now James and Mary had fled to France, but their son, James Edward, was later to play an important part in Scottish history.

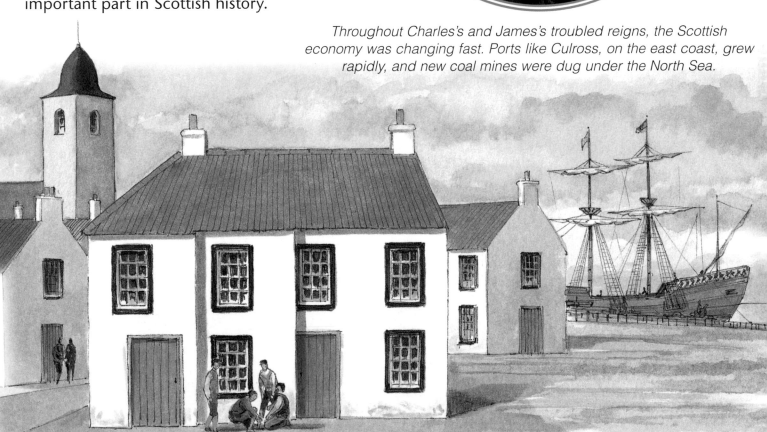

Throughout Charles's and James's troubled reigns, the Scottish economy was changing fast. Ports like Culross, on the east coast, grew rapidly, and new coal mines were dug under the North Sea.

Highland Control

James VII's daughter, Mary, and her Dutch husband, William of Orange, ruled Scotland jointly with England from 1689 to 1702. They were Protestants but believed in religious toleration, and gave Presbyterians freedom to worship so long as Catholics were free as well.

But many Scots – nicknamed "Jacobites" – were troubled. They believed that James VII was their lawful king. They also saw how Scots Presbyterian leaders were very hostile to people who did not share their views. In the Highlands especially, a large number of people living in remote villages had remained Catholic throughout the Reformation and the Covenanting times.

"Bonnie" Dundee

Scottish nobles who supported William and Mary recruited Scottish troops to fight against William's enemies. In 1689 they clashed with a Highlander army led by rebel, Viscount "Bonnie" Dundee. The Jacobite army won but Dundee was killed and the rebellion collapsed.

King William III of England and Scotland. Fort William (opposite page) was named after him.

Mary II of England and Scotland, wife of King William III.

Buying loyalty

The government of William and Mary in Scotland now faced a big problem. How could they stop Scotland being damaged by yet another war? And how could they stop France – Scotland's ally but England's enemy – helping the Jacobites? They offered Highland chiefs large sums of money if they signed a pledge of loyalty to William and Mary by 1 January, 1692. One leading Highland chief, MacDonald of Glencoe, was five days late in signing. So government ministers decided to make an example of him ...

This 19th-century painting shows one of the English forts built to control Highland Scotland at Fort William in 1655. It was rebuilt, in stone, in 1690.

Massacre at Glencoe

On 13 February, 1692, the chief government minister, Lord Stair, sent a troop of soldiers from the Campbell clan (whose leaders supported King William III) to lodge with MacDonald villagers in Glencoe. Following ancient Highland tradition the MacDonalds welcomed and fed them. But in the night, the Campbells pushed all the MacDonalds – including old people, women and children – out into the bitterly cold snow and murdered 38 of them.

The Campbells and the MacDonalds had been enemies for centuries, but the massacre at Glencoe broke ancient rules of war and shocked all Scotland.

Polite Society

From around 1700, rich families in Scotland began to enjoy a more peaceful, "civilized" way of life.

The massacre at Glencoe continued the Scottish tradition of settling quarrels by violence. But Scotland was slowly changing. A new society was developing, linking many of Scotland's wealthy, powerful families with polite society in England and France. They aimed to leave Scotland's history of bloody clan battles and "primitive" life behind.

In the countryside throughout Scotland, rich nobles and landowners built elegant houses to replace old castles. These homes had smaller, cosier rooms designed for families to live quietly and peacefully – reading books, writing letters, making music, entertaining friends, and hunting, shooting and fishing for sport.

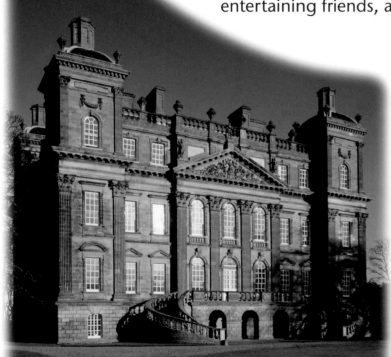

Foreign fashions

These wealthy Scots paid for European artists to paint family portraits. They ate and drank new foods, such as tea, coffee, sugar and chocolate imported from Asia and America. They bought the latest books and newspapers, and sent their sons to study at Scottish and European universities. They travelled to Edinburgh and to London to take part in elegant "assemblies" with music and dancing. Their daughters dressed in the latest English fashions.

Duffus House, in north-east Scotland, was built and enlarged in the 17th and 18th centuries to provide a comfortable, elegant home for a rich Scottish family.

A comfortable life

In towns, rich merchants also built grand houses designed for comfortable, stylish living, away from "working-class" areas where poor people lived, crowded together next to noisy inns and dirty workshops. The largest Scottish town – Edinburgh – now had 30,000 inhabitants. Glasgow was home to around 15,000 people, and Aberdeen and Dundee to around 10,000 each.

Did you know?
While rich people lived comfortably, poor Scots went hungry. The 1690s were famine years in many parts of Scotland.

The smelly, dirty, crowded streets of Edinburgh Old Town, around 1700.

English is best!

There was another very important change in "polite" society. Rich Scottish people, in the Highlands as well as the Lowlands, began to speak English instead of Gaelic or Scots. These old Scottish languages were now seen as "uncouth" or "barbaric" – and suitable for poor, working people only.

Polite Society around 1600–1700

1601	1620	1635	1651	1662	around 1693
Tax on wine (drunk by rich people) "to restrain drunkenness".	First recorded Scottish portrait-painter, George Jamesone of Aberdeen.	First postal service between Edinburgh and London.	*Scottish Mercury* – first Scottish newspaper.	Laws against "barbarous" Gaelic language.	First public concerts in Edinburgh.

New Enterprises

Scotland's new "polite" society needed money to sustain its comfortable lifestyle. Mostly this came from farming. Noble and wealthy Scottish families, including Highland chiefs, owned most of the country's land.

But in Scotland's fast-growing towns, some enterprising people were aiming to make their fortunes in daring new business ventures. Sometimes these succeeded – but sometimes they failed, spectacularly.

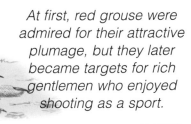

At first, red grouse were admired for their attractive plumage, but they later became targets for rich gentlemen who enjoyed shooting as a sport.

New farming
From around 1650 landowners tried new ways of managing the countryside. They ended community-based farming in which all villagers grew a mixture of crops for their own use in common fields. Instead they tried to get the maximum profit from their lands. They increased rents and employed "factors" (estate managers) to collect them. They drained boggy fields, used fertilizers and planted large areas with single crops to sell to towns. They also raised large herds of cattle to export to England.

The Glasford family were tobacco merchants in Glasgow. They commissioned this portrait in 1767.

New industries

There were also changes to Scottish industries. Landowners opened new coal mines and built big, new salt-making factories. City councils invested in commercial developments such as the deep-water harbour at Port Glasgow, opened in 1667. Town businessmen set up distilleries and bonds (warehouses) to make and sell whisky, and rope-works to supply sailing ships. They imported profitable new goods, such as tobacco. They were also slave traders.

In 1695 Scottish merchants set up their own colony in Darien, Panama. But Darien was so hot and disease-ridden that the colony was eventually abandoned after more than 2,000 settlers died. The merchants lost all their money.

Economic crisis

But English wars against the French disrupted Scotland's trade, and neighbouring countries like England and the Netherlands imposed heavy taxes on imports of Scottish coal. Wet weather ruined harvests, leading to famine in Scotland from 1695 to 1699.

In 1672 and 1681 the Scottish government passed laws to encourage trade and protect industries. But these were not enough. Some poor people emigrated, or left Scotland to fight as professional soldiers. Many others invested in the exciting but risky "Darien Scheme". It was a disaster!

Act of Union

By 1702 James VII, Queen Mary and William of Orange had all died. The next queen of Scotland (and England) was Mary's sister, Anne. During her reign, two major events took place that changed Scotland for ever.

In 1707 the Scottish Parliament was closed down (and did not resume for almost 300 years). The same year, Scotland stopped being an independent country and united with England.

Queen Anne receives the Act of Union (law uniting Scotland with England), 1707.

Trade and security

Why did this union take place? There were two main reasons. Anne's government, like that of William and Mary before, wanted to keep tight control over all the British Isles. The English Parliament also wanted to stop Prince James Edward (the son of exiled James VII) using Scotland as a base from which to claim the English and Scottish crowns. The prince still had many Jacobite supporters in Scotland. They called him James VIII; the English called him "the Old Pretender".

Who should be king?

Discussions about the Union began in 1702 but were held up by quarrels about trade. The English wanted to keep Scots away from all their overseas lands. The Scots said this was unfair. The Scots also wanted freedom to choose their own religion – and their own king. In particular, Jacobite Scots disagreed with the English Parliament's choice of ruler after Anne's death. He was a German prince, George of Hanover, a great-grandson of Scottish King James VI.

The rebellion of 1715

Queen Anne died in 1714 and George was declared king. The next year Scottish Jacobites rebelled. Prince James Edward set sail from France with a promise from French King Louis XIV to send men and ships to support him. But Louis died and help never arrived. Before James even landed in Scotland, Jacobite troops fought an English army at Sherrifmuir in 1715. Neither side won but the Jacobites suffered more. James Edward stayed in Scotland for about a month then sailed back to France in 1716. His rebellion had failed.

The Earl of Mar raised the royal standard at Braemar in 1715 to show his support for Prince James Edward.

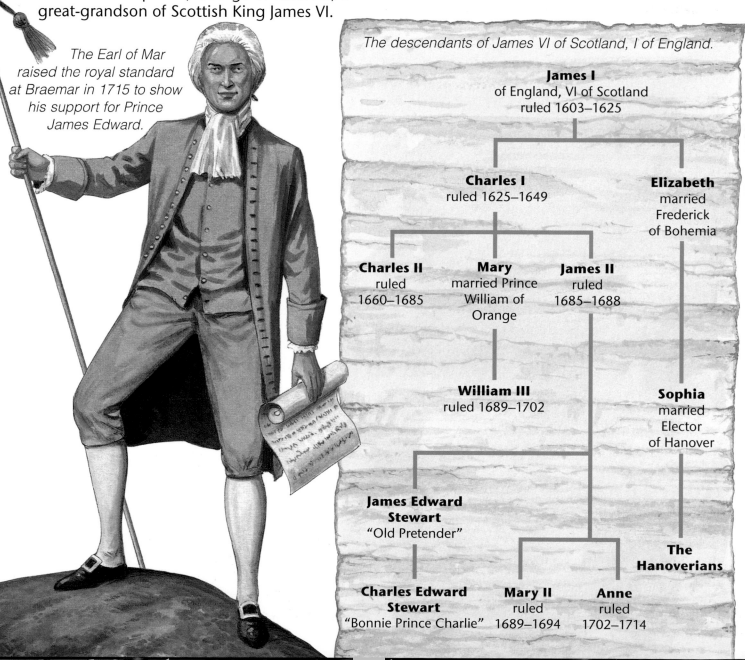

The descendants of James VI of Scotland, I of England.

James I
of England, VI of Scotland
ruled 1603–1625

Charles I
ruled 1625–1649

Elizabeth
married Frederick of Bohemia

Charles II
ruled 1660–1685

Mary
married Prince William of Orange

James II
ruled 1685–1688

William III
ruled 1689–1702

Sophia
married Elector of Hanover

James Edward Stewart
"Old Pretender"

The Hanoverians

Charles Edward Stewart
"Bonnie Prince Charlie"

Mary II
ruled 1689–1694

Anne
ruled 1702–1714

The Jacobites – 1745

After the 1715 Jacobite rebellion, the English government punished Scots who had taken part by confiscating their estates or transporting them to America. The ringleaders were executed.

Even so, some Scots continued to call for an end to the Union. They claimed that their economy was being wrecked by English taxes and English traders. They felt angry that Presbyterians could still not worship freely, and believed that the English government did not care about the Scottish people or the Scottish state.

Prince Charles Edward, 1720–1788, son of Prince James Edward and grandson of King James VII and II.

The Young Pretender

The Scots complained that English kings, George I and his son George II, backed policies only to suit England. They did not like the new "sheriffs" (regional law officers) introduced by the English to control the Scots countryside, or the English soldiers stationed in the Highlands.

The Jacobites planned a third rebellion, helped by Spain, in 1719. It failed after a storm scattered the Spanish fleet. But by 1744 the Jacobites had a new leader, James Edward's son, Charles. The Scots hailed him as "Bonnie Prince Charlie". The English called him "the Young Pretender".

A Scots noblewoman, Flora MacDonald, helped Prince Charlie escape after his rebellion failed.

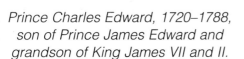

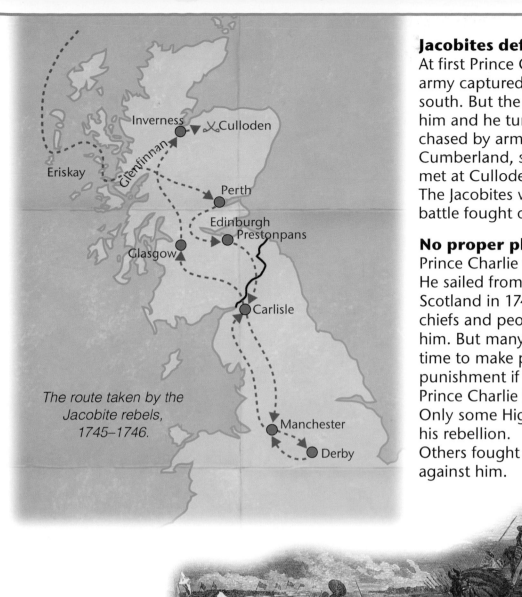

The route taken by the Jacobite rebels, 1745–1746.

Jacobites defeated

At first Prince Charlie was successful. His army captured Edinburgh then headed south. But the English would not support him and he turned back to the Highlands, chased by army commander "Butcher" Cumberland, son of George II. Their armies met at Culloden, near Inverness, in 1746. The Jacobites were massacred. It was the last battle fought on British soil.

No proper plans

Prince Charlie was full of romantic dreams. He sailed from France to the west of Scotland in 1745, convinced that local chiefs and people would hurry to support him. But many did not. They had not had time to make proper plans and they feared punishment if caught. And they knew that Prince Charlie had no experience of fighting. Only some Highland clans joined his rebellion. Others fought against him.

The Jacobites were massacred at the battle of Culloden, 16 April, 1746.

After the Rebellion of 1745

1746	1746	1746	1746	1748
Prince Charlie lives rough in the hills.	Prince Charlie escapes, helped by Flora MacDonald.	Cumberland's troops ransack the Highlands.	English government bans kilts, plaid and bagpipes!	New laws to end powers of clan chiefs.

Edinburgh Enlightenment

The city of Edinburgh was Scotland's capital. After 1707 it remained the centre of Scottish law and religion but it was no longer the centre of Scottish government. Nobles, officials and other powerful Scottish people now spent more time in London. As a result, life in the city changed dramatically.

After around 1750, new people moved to live in Edinburgh – artists, architects, designers, writers, printers, publishers, booksellers, scientists, scholars, teachers and students. All these lively minded people met together in coffee houses, private clubs, public lectures and assemblies, and "salons" (social gatherings hosted by intelligent, fashionable women). They set up Scotland's first lending library and its first medical school.

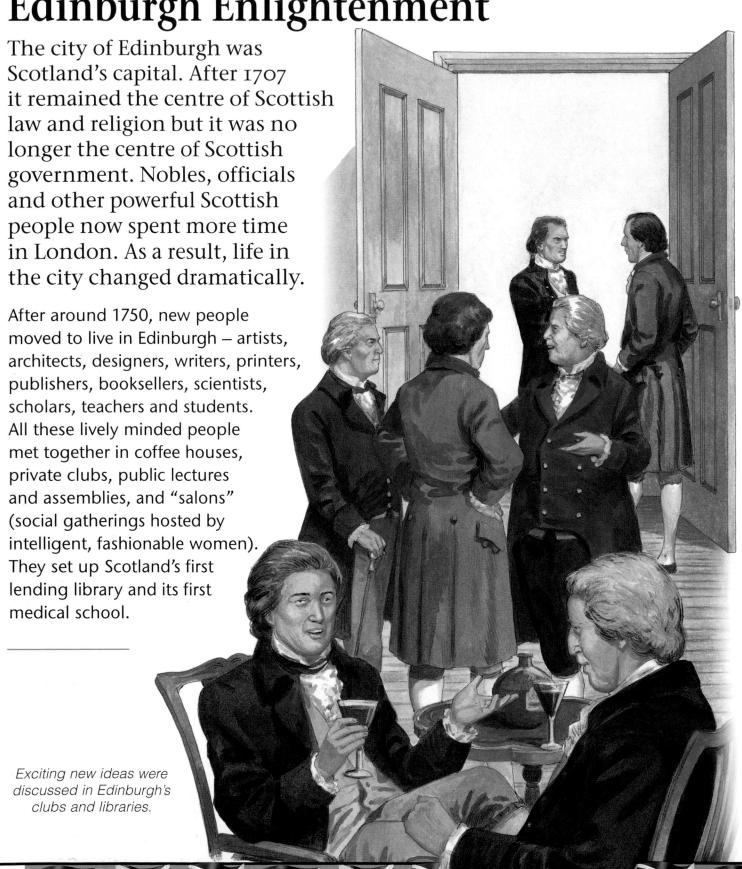

Exciting new ideas were discussed in Edinburgh's clubs and libraries.

Edinburgh's "New Town"

There were also many new buildings in Edinburgh itself. In 1751 a city survey revealed that many streets in the town were crowded, dirty and unhealthy. So the city leaders planned an exclusive residential district for people "of a certain rank and fortune only". No shops or businesses or "places of entertainment" were allowed there. Building work on this new development began in 1767. Straight away, Edinburgh's "New Town" attracted admiring visitors. By 1800, however, the old town had become a slum.

Charlotte Square in Edinburgh's New Town was designed by famous Scottish architect, Robert Adam, in 1791.

This portrait of his wife was painted by Allan Ramsay around 1760.

A good education

Many of Edinburgh's "new people" came from ordinary families. But they had received a good education from Scotland's pioneer public education system. They produced exciting, controversial books and newspapers, discussing the latest ideas in science, politics, economics and philosophy. Painters like Allan Ramsay created beautiful paintings. Architects like Robert Adam designed impressive buildings for clients throughout the United Kingdom.

Scottish Education before 1800

1549
Catholic Church in Scotland calls for "a school in every parish".

1560
Church of Scotland calls for schools for girls as well as boys.

1633, 1646, 1696
Scottish Parliament votes extra money to pay for parish schools.

1700
Nine out of ten Scottish parishes now have schools.

1760s
Many towns have "academies", teaching latest technology.

1790
Almost all Scots can now read, write and do simple maths.

Many cotton factories were built in the Lowlands regions, and were hot, steamy and noisy places to work.

Engineers and Inventors

The Scottish educational system encouraged pupils to study the latest technology, as well as old-fashioned Greek and Latin languages taught in English schools.

Books and newspapers published in Edinburgh spread information about pioneering experiments and exciting discoveries in subjects ranging from farming and geography, to chemistry and maths. Scotland's links with France also kept Scots scholars in touch with the latest European philosophical ideas.

New industries

Around the same time, a new industry – iron-making – was growing up in Scotland. The first Scottish blast furnace was built in 1610 in the Highlands. It used charcoal from local forests to smelt iron ore. In the Lowlands region, businessmen also set up experimental workshops to make glass, paper, porcelain, fine woollen cloth and gunpowder, and built refineries to process sugar imported from the Caribbean.

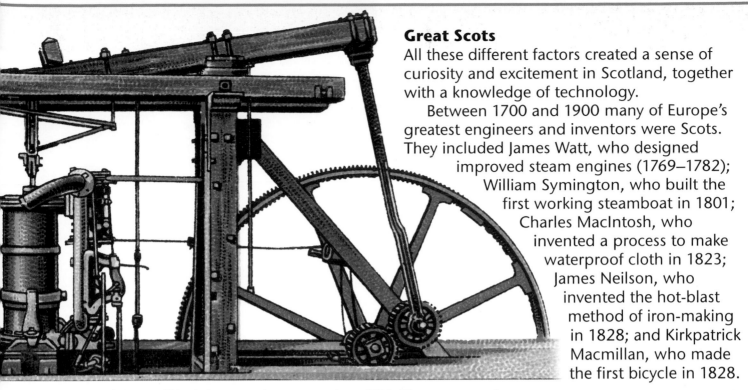

Great Scots

All these different factors created a sense of curiosity and excitement in Scotland, together with a knowledge of technology.

Between 1700 and 1900 many of Europe's greatest engineers and inventors were Scots. They included James Watt, who designed improved steam engines (1769–1782); William Symington, who built the first working steamboat in 1801; Charles MacIntosh, who invented a process to make waterproof cloth in 1823; James Neilson, who invented the hot-blast method of iron-making in 1828; and Kirkpatrick Macmillan, who made the first bicycle in 1828.

A model of James Watt's improved steam engine, 1789. The steam engine provided power for many new industries throughout the United Kingdom.

Old technologies

Scotland also had a long tradition of small-scale technology. For centuries, Scottish miners had been tunnelling underground to dig coal to export to England, burn in household fires and use in local industries, such as burning lime (used for fertilizer and to make mortar) and making salt. After around 1600, Scottish mines grew larger, and one, near Culross, Fife, extended 2.5 kilometres (1.6 miles) out under the sea-bed.

The world's first working paddle-steamer, the Charlotte Dundas, *was built in Scotland in 1801. It was designed by William Symington.*

Industrial Revolution

Scottish engineers and inventors changed the world by helping to create the first Industrial Revolution. From around 1750–1850, millions of ordinary men and women worldwide stopped working at home, on farms or in small craft workshops, and began to work in huge factories.

These factories housed machines that could mass-produce items more quickly and cheaply than any human worker. The earliest machines in Scotland spun and wove cotton thread. Scots also specialized in metal goods – from baths and cooking pots, to ships and weapons. Scotland also exported vast amounts of iron (made in foundries) and coal.

Did you know?
Large numbers of people migrated from Ireland to find work in Scotland's industries. In 1841, 16 per cent of Glasgow's population (44,000 people) had been born in Ireland.

Robert Owen created a new village with factories, homes and schools for Scottish workers. He called it New Lanark.

Millworkers at New Lanark, around 1890.

Industrial zone
At first, machines were driven by fast-flowing water but after around 1800 many were powered by steam. Most were set up in the Central Region where there was plenty of water, coal to heat it to make steam, and rock containing iron. International ports, where cotton to spin was offloaded, were not far away. Many people lived in the region already, working in small foundries and mines. Others migrated there from poor Lowland and Highland countryside.

The first direct Glasgow to London stage-coach service began in 1788. Improved road surfaces designed by MacAdam made long road journeys much safer and faster.

Rapid growth

In the early years of the Industrial Revolution, Scottish industry grew very fast. For example, almost 200 cotton factories were set up between 1778 and 1839. In 1830 the largest chemical works in the world opened in Glasgow. By 1849, Scotland produced a quarter of the United Kingdom's output of iron and over 3 million tonnes of coal a year.

Roads, bridges and canals

Scots engineers made great improvements to transport to carry factory-made goods away to sell. John MacAdam pioneered new methods of road construction. Thomas Telford designed roads, bridges, harbours and the Caledonian Canal. It linked the North Sea and the Atlantic Ocean, and saved a dangerous journey round the north of Scotland. Robert Stevenson designed amazing lighthouses to warn ships of hazards around the coast. Scotland's first steam-powered railway, from Glasgow to Garnkirk, opened in 1826.

Canal boats carried bulky cargoes of raw materials and finished goods to and from Scotland's industrial towns.

Scottish Transport

1713	1722	1750s–1760s	1768–1790	1803–1847	1812
First new turnpike road built. New stage-coach services.	First Scottish tramway, in colliery.	First Scottish colliery "railways", on wooden tracks, pulled by horses.	First canal (Forth and Clyde) links east and west Scotland.	Telford builds Caledonian Canal, and many roads and bridges.	Europe's first steamboat service operates on River Clyde.

Sheep and Seaweed

While Scotland's first industries were developing, many changes were also taking place in the countryside – especially in the Highlands – as landowners became increasingly keen to make more money from their estates.

New crops, such as turnips and potatoes, were planted in enclosed fields surrounded by dry-stone walls. New, business-like farm managers used new machines to cultivate the land, and reap (cut) and thresh (separate seeds from stalks) grain crops. Vast numbers of cattle were reared on rough grassland and driven to Lowland markets to be sold. They were then driven south to provide meat for workers in English towns.

New uses for the countryside
New forests were planted on mountain slopes to produce timber to build new towns. New quarries were cut in mountain-sides to provide building stone and slates for roofing. Large areas were set aside from cultivation to use for stalking deer, for rich families' sport, and to raise newly introduced Blackface sheep.

Landowners introduced hardy Blackface sheep to their Scottish estates. They were more profitable than cattle or poor tenant farmers.

The Clearances
Estate-owners soon found that sheep were even more profitable than cattle-rearing or collecting money from the Scottish people who rented small farms on their land. They used threats and brutality to "persuade" many highland families to leave homes where their ancestors had lived for hundreds of years. Thousands of Highlanders were forced to make a horrible choice – to settle on miserable "crofts" (little plots of rocky, barren land) or leave their home country for ever.

Emigration from Scotland increased after 1846–1847, when the Scottish potato crop failed and there was widespread famine, especially in Highland areas.

Crofting life

Most crofts were not large enough to grow food to feed a family. Crofters had to work for low wages on estate-owners' land, or make money from short-term projects such as burning kelp (seaweed) to produce essential chemicals while Britain was at war with France from 1793 to 1815. Large numbers of young men and women left the Highlands to look for work in Lowland Scotland's growing industrial towns. Many others drowned in rotten, leaky, migrant ships as they sailed towards an unknown future in Australia, Canada or the United States of America.

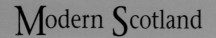

Modern Scotland

In just 100 years, between 1750 and 1850, Scotland was transformed from a poor, rebellious region to the workshop of the world. But the 20th century saw heavy industries decline. And, in 1999, the Scottish Parliament met again, for the first time in almost 300 years.

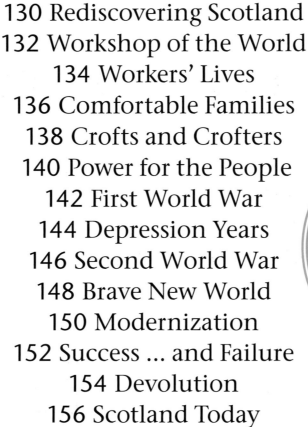

Rediscovering Scotland

After the rebellion of 1745, the government in London was determined to crush the Jacobite problem and "tame" the Highlands for ever. The Gaelic language was banned, along with plaid, Highland weapons and bagpipes. Scotland was run by two Scottish nobles, the Duke of Argyll and Henry Dundas, who obeyed orders from London.

But, after around 1800, attitudes towards Scotland began to change. Scots thinkers, writers, artists, inventors and engineers became greatly respected. New regiments of Scots soldiers in the British army, who were recruited to fight for Britain overseas, also won praise.

Scottish writers

There were new fashions in art, poetry and leisure, south of the border. Readers now enjoyed books by Scottish writers such as Sir Walter Scott, who told tales of Scottish heroes, and the young, handsome poet, Robert Burns. His works blended old Scottish myths and legends with love stories.

Savage or sublime?

Clever, artistic people began to look at Scotland's rugged landscape as not "savage" but "sublime". Some southerners even saw Highlanders in a romantic light, as an ancient, heroic people. In 1821 King George IV became the first British king to visit Scotland in 171 years. He said he liked it.

When King George IV visited Scotland he wore a kilt as a compliment to the country. But, behaving modestly, he added pale-pink woollen tights underneath.

Royal favourite

The greatest admirer of Scotland was probably Queen Victoria herself. She came to the throne in 1837 after George IV's brother, William IV, died. Victoria visited Scotland soon afterwards with her husband, Prince Albert. They built a Scottish-style castle at Balmoral, in north-east Scotland, as their holiday home and began a fashion among rich families for Scottish holidays, deer-stalking and tartan. After Albert died, Victoria consoled herself with long visits to the Highlands – and attracted a great deal of gossip by becoming close friends with a Highland servant, John Brown.

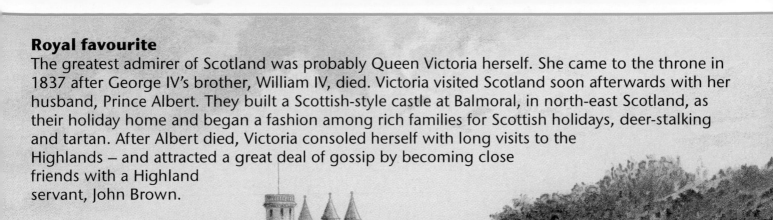

Balmoral Castle was built using granite from the nearby quarries of Glen Gelder, which produced an almost-white stone.

Did you know?
For their holidays, factory-owners and other rich businessmen liked to cruise round the coast of Scotland in huge, expensive pleasure boats. Steam yachts (graceful sailing ships, fitted with motors) were the favourite.

Queen Victoria, seen here on horseback with her servant John Brown, set the fashion among wealthy people for Scottish Highland holidays.

Workshop of the World

While rich, fashionable people were enjoying the Highlands, Lowland Scotland was changing very rapidly. Between 1800 and 1850 the Central Region of the Lowlands, between Edinburgh and Glasgow, became one of the most industrialized places in the world.

Lowland Scotland already had a tradition of small-scale industry based on coal, iron and linen-weaving. But after around 1780 many large, new factories were built there with steam-powered machines to spin wool and cotton thread, and weave them into cloth. In the 1840s new factories in Dundee made cloth from a plant fibre called jute. It was used for sacks, and in floorings and furnishings.

In the first half of the 19th century, Scottish industry grew rapidly, and mining became an important part of Scotland's economy.

Heavy industry

Throughout the Central Region of Lowland Scotland there were also mines, coke-ovens, gas works, iron furnaces, steelworks, engineering workshops, shipbuilding yards, locomotive works and chemical factories – together with industrial-scale food production plants, especially breweries.

Scottish achievements

Scottish workers made the world's first paddle-steamer, iron-hulled passenger ship, reaping machine, screw propeller, steam hammer, pneumatic tyre and linoleum. They also made many great iron bridges, lock-gates (for canals), beams and girders (used to build factories) and iron pipes (for water and drains), plus millions of iron ranges (fires and ovens) used in 19th-century homes. They built thousands of massive steam locomotives and countless miles of rails for them to travel on.

The Forth Rail Bridge, in east-central Scotland, was a triumph of 19th-century engineering. Opened in 1890, it was 2.5 kilometres (8,202 feet) long with a tower height of 100 metres (330 feet).

Foreign profits

Many Scottish goods were produced for export. They were carried away from Scotland by ship and railway to be sold in England, America or British-ruled colonies overseas. Much of the wealth created by this industry also left Scotland. It was passed to owners and share-holders in industrial companies, many of whom were based in England. Although Scottish workers flocked to fast-growing towns in the early 19th century to escape from poverty in the countryside, Scottish workers' wages were, on average, lower than English ones.

Many of Scotland's biggest cities, such as Dundee, were also busy ports. Ships arrived there from British Empire lands, bringing raw materials for industry, such as jute (an Asian plant fibre used to make sacks and carpets).

Workers' Lives

By 1851 one out of five Scots lived in just four big cities – Glasgow, Edinburgh, Dundee and Aberdeen. But citizens' lives were not all the same. A survey made in 1867 revealed that there was a great gap between Scotland's rich and poor.

Seven out of every 10 Scottish people belonged to the working class. Although they laboured for up to 14 hours per day, their wages were very low. Their jobs were dirty and dangerous, and this made many of them weak and sick. If they were injured they could not work or earn. In times of economic slowdown they might be laid off work with no pay.

In tenement homes, families had no space, little comfort and no privacy. There were no curtains or carpets either.

Industrial zones

Scottish workers lived in inner-city districts and in industrial zones close to the places where they worked. They rented rooms in tenement buildings or in communal lodging houses.

Tenements were tall apartment blocks, several storeys high. Most rooms had a single cold-water tap but few had lavatories. Occupants used a shared toilet in the tenement backyard. Many rooms had a fireplace but families could not always afford fuel. There was no gas or electricity. Lighting came from candles or oil lamps.

Overcrowding

Tenements could be damp and noisy, and were always very crowded. There was no privacy. A survey in 1861 found that one-third of Scottish families lived in just one room and another third had only two. Overcrowding in Scottish cities was six times worse than in English cities.

A poor street in Glasgow, around 1900. Many thousands of Scottish workers lived in homes like these.

Once a week, poor women took their family's laundry to a communal wash-house, called a "steamie". Here, they scrubbed and rinsed dirty clothes, sheets and towels by hand – while gossiping with their friends.

Miserable lives

Families, especially women, worked hard to keep clean, tidy and respectable in such conditions, but the stresses were enormous. To escape the pressures of hard work, low pay and poor housing, many men drank too much alcohol and some families made the risky decision to emigrate. Those who remained were at constant risk from infectious diseases. On average, one in eight babies died.

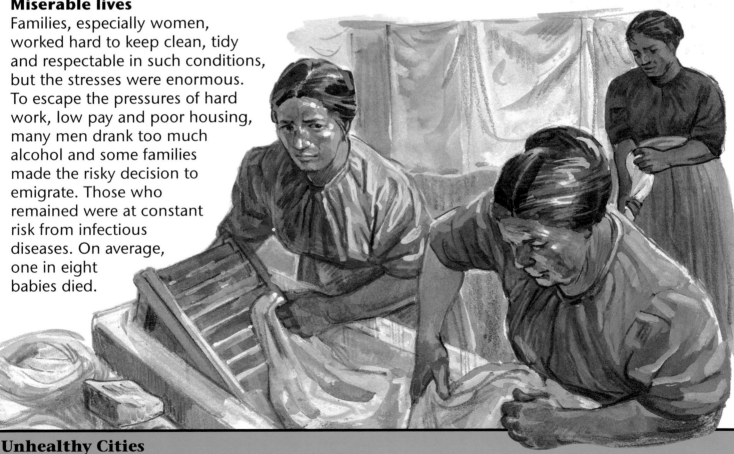

Unhealthy Cities

1832, 1848, 1853, 1866
Epidemics of cholera kill thousands in cities.

1842
Report finds poverty, dirt and disease in city lodgings.

1845
Poor Law (Scotland) Act provides basic medical care for poor.

1866
Glasgow city laws try to limit over-crowding in tenements.

1867
New Public Health (Scotland) Act to improve water, drains and disease control.

1875
Artisans' and Labourers' Dwellings Act improves standards for workers' homes.

Comfortable Families

While the majority of Scottish citizens led hard, unpleasant lives, others had a much more comfortable existence. They belonged to the middle class. In addition, a tiny minority of city-dwellers – only 3 in 1,000 – were upper class. But they often spent much of the year out of town on their country estates.

Middle-class families were not all the same. Upper middle-class people (about 1 in 10 of the city population) included well-paid professionals such as lawyers and doctors, top churchmen and wealthy businessmen. They were often very rich. Together with the upper class, this top 10 per cent of Scottish society had almost 50 per cent of the nation's wealth.

Well educated

Lower middle-class people (about 2 in 10 of city-dwellers) included skilled workers such as draughtsmen and engineers, clerks and other office workers, and small shopkeepers. They were well trained and often well educated. Many had served apprenticeships and continued their studies after work at night schools run by organizations such as the Workers' Educational Association.

Smart areas in cities began to develop around 1900, as shown here in Edinburgh.

Women at home

Middle-class women mostly stayed at home, managing their houses and organizing their servants. They took an interest in fashionable clothes and furnishings, and went shopping in smart new stores. They supervised their children's education, entertained their husbands' business colleagues, and helped raise funds for churches or local charities, or to build new schools and colleges. A few took an interest in controversial issues such as women's education, career opportunities or voting rights.

Leisure time

Unlike working-class people, middle-class families had more opportunities for leisure and more money to enjoy it. They visited the splendid new museums and libraries built in Scotland's big cities and towns, and enjoyed parties, dances and performances at theatres and concert halls.

Middle-class families could afford to furnish their homes in fashionable style. In the mid-19th century, the fashion was for rich curtains and carpets, patterned wallpapers and plenty of pictures and ornaments.

Respectable citizens

During the 19th century, Scottish middle-class people moved to live in new residential districts, often on the outskirts of big cities. Men travelled to work by new public transport, such as railways and trams. They joined business associations, clubs and debating societies, took part in politics and served on town councils.

By around 1900, fashions in house design changed. The plain, elegant "art nouveau" (new art) style, pioneered in Scotland by architect Charles Rennie Mackintosh, became popular.

Crofts and Crofters

During the Clearances, thousands of Highland families moved to big Lowland cities. Thousands more emigrated. But what happened to those who were left behind?

Most became crofters. Their landlords allowed them to rent small plots of land called "crofts". Usually these were sited on stony or boggy ground, or right on the seashore. They were not big enough to provide food for a family – even if crofters grew potatoes. This was their favourite crop because potatoes provided four times more food value than grain.

Hard work

Landowners kept croft plots deliberately small and poor so that crofters would have to work for them as farm-hands, house servants and ghillies. To make a little more money, crofting men also went fishing. Crofting women purchased wool and wove it by hand into a new, fashionable cloth called "tweed".

Potato famine

But in 1846 disaster struck. Crofters' potato crops caught a disease called blight and rotted away. The British government sent emergency food supplies – by new steam-powered "puffers" (small cargo ships) – but many families almost starved. Still more Highlanders had to leave their homelands.

Many crofters lived in small, damp, dark cottages, built of rough stone and thatched with heather.

Crofters dug peat from the land to burn as fuel.

Many Highland families made a living from fishing. The fishing port of Mallaig, on the north-west coast, sent hundreds of boxes of fish south to Glasgow and England every day.

Fighting for crofters' rights

Landlords and crofters disliked and distrusted each other. In the 1880s these bitter feelings turned to war. It began when crofters in Skye asked to rent more land to keep more animals. When the landlord refused they staged a rent strike. In return, the landlord obtained court orders to turn them off their crofts. But the crofters refused to leave.

The British government sent police and marines, but the crofters, including many women, fought back in the "Battle of the Braes" (11 April, 1882). Crofters who took part were put on trial but let off with very small fines because, in many parts of Britain, public opinion was on their side. The government set up a committee to make new, fairer rules for renting croft land. The laws they made – although updated in 1886 – still govern many parts of Highland Scotland today.

Did you know?
To escape poverty in the Scottish countryside, around 27,000 Scottish men, women and children emigrated between 1760 and 1815, and an astonishing 1.9 million between 1815 and 1914.

Power for the People

Scottish workers were tough, but most felt powerless. Throughout the 19th century, ordinary men and women did not have the right to vote. They could not choose their political leaders or make their views known. Scottish country lairds (rich landowners) controlled their tenants' wages, work and cottages. In cities, unelected councils controlled housing and public health.

To protest, some Scottish men and women joined trades unions to campaign for better wages and working conditions. They took part in demonstrations demanding political reform. In 1820 clashes between police, reformers and poor workers were so violent that they were called the "Radical Wars". Later, political protests were organized by groups such as the Chartists, who also campaigned in England.

Made for the Amalgamated Society (trade union) of Railway Servants for Scotland, this banner carries the slogans "Union is strength" and "All men are brethren" (brothers).

Between 1836 and 1848, the Chartists called for Parliamentary reform and the right to vote for all men. They staged peaceful protests, such as sit-ins in churches, seen here in this 19th-century engraving.

Ladies who campaigned for voting rights for women were known as "suffragettes".

EDINBURGH

Religious problems

There were calls for reform of Scotland's religion at this time. Most Scottish people belonged to the Protestant Church of Scotland – though in the north-west and the industrial Lowlands many people were Roman Catholics.

Church of Scotland members quarrelled over who should appoint ministers to lead them – ordinary church people or local lairds. In 1733 protesters wanting to choose their own ministers set up a new Secession Church. In 1761 more breakaways founded the Relief Church. Finally, in 1843, 400 rebel Church of Scotland ministers formed another, new church – the Free Church.

United and free

The Free Church became very popular, especially in the Highlands. Within five years it had over 700 churches, 500 schools, a college and two missionary societies. Members chose their own ministers and insisted that no work, travel or play should take place on Sundays. By 1929 the three breakaway churches joined together to form the United Free Church.

Limited reforms

In 1833 Scottish town councils were also reformed, making them less corrupt and more democratic. The British Parliament passed laws to improve conditions in factories and appointed more Scottish MPs. But over half of all Scots men still did not have the vote.

Democratic Progress

1832	1833	1868, 1885	1888	1887	1918
Wealthy men given right to vote. More Scots MPs created.	Town councils reformed; become more democratic.	Around half of all working men win the right to vote.	Scottish Labour Party formed.	Scottish Trades Union Congress founded.	All men win the right to vote. (Most women have to wait until 1928.)

First World War

Between 1800 and 1900 Scotland was transformed. Its population more than doubled to over four million. Over half of all Scottish people now lived in towns in the Central Lowlands. Glasgow, with a population of over one million in 1901, boasted it was "the second city of the British Empire".

Clydeside, close to Glasgow, was the greatest ship-building area in the world; Scotland was also one of the world's major steam-locomotive builders. Overall, Scottish living conditions had improved and poverty had decreased over the century. But in the Highland region, by 1898, over 2.5 million acres of land was taken up by deer forests (shooting and holiday estates); much more was occupied by sheep. Many crofters were desperately poor.

Scottish soldiers

Further upheavals came at the start of the First World War in 1914, when Britain and its allies declared war on Germany. The fighting lasted until 1918. Thousands of Scottish men were encouraged to volunteer for Scotland's own local regiments. From 1916 they were forced by law to join. In many towns and villages all the young men of fighting age (between around 16 and 40) went to war together – and died together in a single battle or raid.

The Gordon Highlanders, machine gun corps, 1914. The Germans nicknamed the Scots "the ladies from hell" because they fought in their kilts!

Warships based in Scotland patrolled the North Sea to help keep Britain safe. They frequently came under German naval attack.

Tragic slaughter

Fighting in the First World War was so terrible that people called it "the war to end all wars". Troops huddled in flooded, rat-infested trenches (narrow holes in the ground) along the "front line" – the narrow strip of territory in Belgium and northern France where the enemy armies came face to face. Then they attacked with poison gas and explosive shells, or charged "over the top" with bayonets fixed to their rifles. Many thousands were killed by machine-gun bullets or trapped on razor wire.

Over 200,000 Scottish women also played a part in the First World War, by making munitions (guns and explosives).

Front-line life

Scottish troops suffered worst of all in the battle of the Somme, fought in July 1916, when thousands died in a single day. Many Scottish sailors were also killed in battles at sea, or in troop and supply ships sunk by German submarines. In the First World War as a whole, 74,000 Scots men were killed and 150,000 were seriously wounded. That was one in five of the young, fit, male Scottish population.

Socialist protesters clashed with troops and police in Glasgow's central George Square on 31 January, 1919. The day became known as "Black Friday".

Depression Years

The First World War placed a great strain on Scotland. Men and women who stayed at home to make weapons and warships worked extra hard, for low wages, while their employers made vast profits by supplying the government.

As the prices of food, clothes and housing rose faster than wages, workers went on strike, demanding better pay; there was also a rent strike by poor Glasgow families. These protests were encouraged by new, socialist political movements, including trades unions and the Communist Party. Support for the Labour Party, founded in 1906, grew among Scottish workers.

Unemployed and unhealthy

After the War, the need for weapons, ships and the steel to make them fell sharply. Scottish company owners had not made plans to reorganize their businesses and so many workers lost their jobs. To make matters worse, around one-quarter of all Scots still lived in unhealthy homes. Thousands of children suffered from rickets (bent bones) caused by poor nutrition, or died from a deadly disease called tuberculosis.

On the dole

Jobless people in cities just managed to survive on government welfare benefits called "the dole". Country-dwellers scavenged for wild food. Housewives everywhere took a pride in making the best use of the cheapest ingredients, recycled old clothes and "kept up appearances". Men took whatever work they could find. Children were encouraged to study to have a better chance of finding a job. But, in spite of these efforts, many Scottish families led cold, hard and hungry lives.

In 1929, hundreds of unemployed Scottish workers took part in "hunger marches" to London, to demand jobs and emergency food aid.

Despite these economic problems, many Scottish people stayed cheerful. They enjoyed watching films and going to dance halls.

Crisis years

In 1929 the American Stock Market crashed, and many businesses became worthless. This caused economic panic all round the world, and a deep crisis in Scotland. On average, one in every three workers became unemployed. In towns where a few factories employed nearly all the workers, almost everyone was without a job. There was also a slump in farming.

Second World War

In 1939, Britain and its allies went to war with Germany again. Fighting in the Second World War lasted until 1945. Young Scottish men and, for the first time, Scottish women were conscripted (forced by law) to join the army and navy – and the new air force.

Once again Scottish industries began to increase production of coal, steel and warships. As in the First World War, many women worked hard, replacing men in engineering works and weapons factories, and driving buses, lorries and trams. Many new airstrips were built in Scotland, together with army and airforce bases where American troops could stay while preparing to fight in Europe.

Commandos training in Scotland learned how to attack enemy targets on daring "undercover" raids.

Tough training

Tough British Commando soldiers received training in the Scottish Highlands before setting off on dangerous missions in enemy lands. Prisoners of war and "enemy aliens" (foreigners whom the British government did not trust) were sent to Scotland and made to work in forestry plantations and on farms.

Civilian deaths

Many fewer servicemen were killed between 1939 and 1945 than during the First World War. However, the total of 36,000 dead still left many grieving parents, wives, girlfriends and children. Scotland's civilians also suffered badly. Around 6,000 men, women and children were killed during the War and thousands more were injured. Many were caught in bombing raids. German aircraft attacked suddenly by night, dropping explosives on dockyards and city homes.

The Fire Guard for the government offices in Edinburgh, 1939 to 1945.

Atlantic convoys

Scotland's position, between the Atlantic Ocean and the North Sea, made it an ideal site for navy dockyards. Warships from Scottish bases patrolled the icy seas, keeping watch for invaders. This was especially important after 1940 when German troops captured Norway, and threatened to attack Britain from the north.

Throughout the war Scottish merchant seamen played a vital part in running convoys of ships in the Atlantic. These brought essential supplies of food and fuel to Britain and to its allies, especially Russia, in the far north of Europe. They faced constant danger of attack by "wolf-packs" of German U-boats (submarines), and thousands drowned.

> **Did you know?**
> Up to 500 Scots per week were moved to England by the government between 1939 and 1945. This was partly because they were needed as workers in new, English, aircraft-making factories.

The ruins of the Dalmuir Tramway Terminus, during the Clydesbank Blitz, 1941.

Brave New World

The Second World War made many British people – including the Scots – look at life in a new way. They met troops from the USA and the Commonwealth, and admired their free-and-easy manners and positive, "can-do" attitude.

British people met refugees from Nazi Europe, who were often artistic and well educated. Above all, they met each other. Rich and poor, British people sheltered together from bombing raids, joined the Home Guard and took part in fire-watching patrols. In the armed forces, they trained and fought side by side.

During the War, extra food rations were handed out to the poor from mobile canteens such as this one in Clydesbank, 1941.

Owned by the people, run by the state. Newcraighill colliery, 1 January, 1947 when the National Coal Board flag was raised.

Welfare state

Throughout the 1940s, socialist politicians had been making plans for a "new" Britain. They wanted all citizens to share in the task of rebuilding society, and to benefit from education, welfare benefits and health care, "from the cradle to the grave". In 1945 a new, Labour (socialist) government came to power. It nationalized many of Britain's industries – including Scottish coalfields, steelworks and railway companies – so that their profits would help the country. It also introduced new taxes to pay for health and welfare.

Food for all

As some of Britain's poorest citizens, Scots welcomed these new plans. They had already seen how government schemes could help them. During the Second World War, the government rationed (limited) the amount of essential foods, such as eggs or cheese, that people were allowed to buy each week. It also controlled the prices of many other foods. In this way, all citizens got enough food to survive, whether they were rich or poor.

Out of date?

Even so, Scotland still faced problems. Many of its biggest industrial plants were now old and out-dated. They needed to be replaced – so did some of their managers, who were out of touch with the new world after the War. Returning soldiers, sailors and airmen needed to find work. But, by 1950, Scottish unemployment levels were twice as high as those in the rest of Britain. In London and in Scotland, government ministers – who now ran most of Scotland's industries – urgently looked for new ideas.

Scottish companies were proud of their traditional skills. But many of them failed to make plans for new products for the future.

Welfare State

1940	1944	1945	1948	1951
Food rationing introduced; free milk for pregnant women and school children.	Education Act provides free secondary education for all; school-leaving age now 15.	Labour Party wins election; promises welfare reforms.	National Health Service and National Insurance Scheme (Social Security) introduced.	Local authority builds first tower-blocks in Glasgow to rehouse people living in slums.

An aerial view of Cumbernauld New Town, around 1980.

Modernization

From the 1940s to the late 1970s, British government ministers worked hard to bring new businesses to Scotland. They were helped by owners of Scottish companies and by Scottish trade unions.

They hoped to create new jobs, make people richer, and build a new, modern Scottish society. City councils also began ambitious schemes to replace old slums with modern tower-blocks, and to build carefully planned new towns.

Water, trees and oil

The first new industries were based on Highland resources, such as mountain lochs (lakes) and fast-growing evergreen trees. Lochs were dammed, and their water was channelled to power turbines (machines generating electricity) and aluminium smelters. Trees produced timber for building, and wood-pulp for paper-making.

In 1959 oil and natural gas were discovered off the north-east coast of Scotland. Later, more oil was found close to the Shetland Isles. This led to a boom in northern Scotland among companies that built drilling rigs, transport ships and pipelines, and created some well-paid jobs for skilled workers.

Scottish workers braved dangerous conditions on massive oil rigs, built far out into the North Sea.

New industries

Further south in Scotland, powerful American companies were asked to set up factories. They made electrical goods, tyres and building machinery. Their factories were sited in the central Lowlands, where most Scottish workers lived. British companies also set up large new plants there, making rolled steel and motor vehicles.

Did you know?
After 1945, many Scottish cities grew smaller, as old industries collapsed and people moved away in search of work. Only Aberdeen, centre of the oil industry, and the new towns – East Kilbride, Irvine, Glenrothes, Livingston and Cumbernauld – grew quickly.

The Americans set up nuclear submarine bases in Scotland, including Holy Loch which remained an active base until recently.

Nuclear energy

To improve communications with the United States and Europe, wartime airfields were converted for use by peace-time cargo and passenger planes. More controversially, old dockyards became bases for British and American nuclear weapons, including submarines. A large experimental nuclear research station was also built in the far north of Scotland.

Help from Europe

In 1973, Britain joined the "Common Market" (now called the European Union). Grants from Europe were used to build new roads and bridges; farmers and remote communities received aid. But many fishermen objected to European environmental rules that limited their catch, and they protested.

Changing Scotland

1947	1948	1956	1959	1960–1961	1960s
East Kilbride is Scotland's first new town; new civil airport at Prestwick.	First hydro-electric schemes open.	First nuclear power station in Scotland.	Oil and gas discovered under the North Sea.	American nuclear submarine base set up at Holy Loch.	Closure of collieries, ironworks and shipyards. New steel- and car-making plants planned.

Success ... and Failure

As new towns and factories were being built, Scottish people also became more proud of Scotland's traditions. It was fashionable to like Scottish folk music and to admire ancient Scotland's historic heritage. Scots enjoyed the fame and prestige brought by the Edinburgh Festival, and by books and films on Scottish themes. In the Highlands, they celebrate the National Mod (Gaelic music and poetry festival).

Scotland was also successful at sport. Racing drivers Jim Clark and Jackie Stewart became world champions – three times each. Scottish boxers and snooker players won honours. Scottish football teams were also successful: in 1967 Celtic became the first British team to win the European Cup; and Scotland also reached the World Cup finals in 1986.

The National Mod is held every year in the Highlands and is a celebration of Gaelic music and poetry.

New arrivals

The tourist industry became increasingly important, attracting millions of visitors every year. Some returned, to stay. In 1974, for the first time since the Second World War, more people moved to Scotland than left it.

Scottish football fans paint their faces with the blue-and-white Saltire – Scotland's national flag.

Too expensive

But Scotland's economy was not so successful. Scotland was too far from customers and raw materials, and Scottish workers lacked experience and skills. Companies found it cheaper to site factories in developing regions, such as the Far East.

Rising unemployment

From 1979 a new Conservative government, led by Margaret Thatcher, reduced state aid for Scotland's economy. Many factories had to close. By 1985 Scottish unemployment was the highest it had been since the Second World War.

Unpopular policies

Many Scottish people also felt threatened by new "Thatcherite" policies. They disliked cuts in transport and public services, high unemployment and the growing gap between rich and poor. They especially hated the Poll Tax (a fixed sum collected from every adult, rich or poor).

Conservative policies were meant to cut waste and encourage enterprise. But they offended old Scottish ideas of neighbourliness and co-operation that had helped Scots survive in hard times.

The magnificent firework display above Edinburgh Castle marks the end of the Edinburgh International Festival.

Cultural Pride

1947
First Edinburgh International Festival.

1950
Scottish National Orchestra founded.

1951
First Scottish National Nature Reserve.

1955
First broadcast by Scottish Television.

1960
Six new universities planned.

1990
Glasgow is chosen as European city of culture.

Devolution

In the 19th century, many Scots looked to England for help and protection. But they also feared that their country might be taken over, and lose its Scottish identity.

In 1886 the Scottish Home Rule Association was formed, and then, in 1921, the Scots National League. In 1934 these two groups combined to form the Scottish National Party. Its members called for complete independence.

Did you know?
Scottish nationalists complained that Queen Elizabeth II should be called "Elizabeth I of Scotland", since there had been no earlier Scottish queens called Elizabeth. They set fire to post boxes marked with her royal cipher (sign): "EIIR".

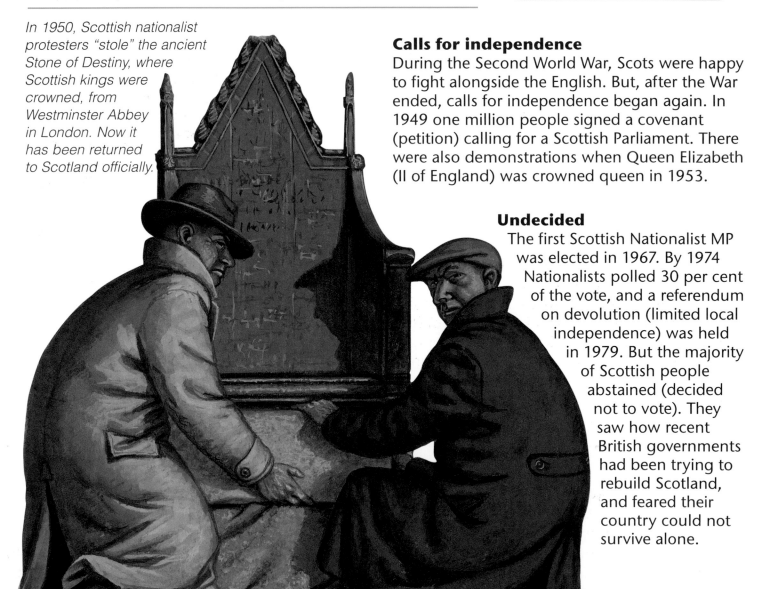

In 1950, Scottish nationalist protesters "stole" the ancient Stone of Destiny, where Scottish kings were crowned, from Westminster Abbey in London. Now it has been returned to Scotland officially.

Calls for independence

During the Second World War, Scots were happy to fight alongside the English. But, after the War ended, calls for independence began again. In 1949 one million people signed a covenant (petition) calling for a Scottish Parliament. There were also demonstrations when Queen Elizabeth (II of England) was crowned queen in 1953.

Undecided

The first Scottish Nationalist MP was elected in 1967. By 1974 Nationalists polled 30 per cent of the vote, and a referendum on devolution (limited local independence) was held in 1979. But the majority of Scottish people abstained (decided not to vote). They saw how recent British governments had been trying to rebuild Scotland, and feared their country could not survive alone.

Unpopular parliament

The new Scottish Parliament held its first meeting in 1999. Since then, the Parliament has been criticized for feeble policies, petty squabbles and poor financial management. The cost of the new parliament building – which has risen tenfold since it was first planned, to over £400 million – has caused public outcry. Some Scots see their Parliament as a waste of time and money. Some think it should have even greater powers. Some are satisfied.

Scots lined the Royal Mile, Edinburgh, when Queen Elizabeth II arrived to open the Scottish Parliament on 1 July, 1999.

Queen Elizabeth II opens the new Scottish Parliament in Edinburgh in 1999 – its first meeting for almost 300 years.

Scotland says "yes"

Eighteen years later, in 1997, a second referendum was held. After years of unpopular policies – and a new pride in Scottish culture – Scottish people voted "yes". In 1998 the new (Labour) British government agreed to bring back the Scottish Parliament, which had not met since 1707, and set up a Scottish Executive with powers to raise (or lower) taxes, and manage Scotland's health care, education, social welfare, transport, farming and the environment .

Scottish Politics

1934
Scottish National Party founded. Demands independence.

1950
Scottish nationalists remove Stone of Destiny from Westminster.

1961
Scottish campaigners call for a referendum on devolution.

1979
Referendum on devolution; majority abstain.

1997
New referendum on devolution; majority in favour.

1999
First Scottish Parliament since 1707 meets. Donald Dewar (1937–2000) is First Minister.

Scotland Today

Today, in the early 21st century, Scotland is a mixture of old and new. Scottish people still feel proud of their country's heritage and identity. They admire its magnificent scenery, wear kilts on special occasions and eat traditional foods such as haggis. Some still speak Scots, the old language of the Lowlands. And, in the Highlands and Islands, children can go to Gaelic-speaking schools.

Yet Scotland is also part of the modern world. Scottish people shop at supermarkets, use mobile phones and watch satellite TV. Scientists at a Scottish research station were the first to clone a mammal – Dolly the sheep – in 1996.

Dolly the sheep (1996–2003) became a media celebrity.

Scotland's largest industry – tourism – is based on Scotland's stunning landscape and rich heritage. It employs over 200,000 people.

New Scots

Scotland also has new inhabitants. Families from the Indian sub-continent have arrived to work or study, along with Africans, Europeans and Japanese. All have brought new ideas or new skills. Recently, Scottish cities have housed refugees from eastern Europe, Afghanistan and the Middle East.

New problems

Sadly, Scotland also has modern problems, including alcohol and drug abuse. In some city districts, there is poverty and vandalism. Scottish farming suffered badly from BSE (so-called "mad cow disease") and foot and mouth disease. Scotland also faces pollution left by earlier industries, especially nuclear power. Since Devolution, Scottish politics has been rocked by scandals – and called "second-rate".

Scotland's first Sikh tartan was created for his Lordship Sirdar Iqbal Singh, Laird of Little Castle, Lesmahagow. He is shown here, wearing a kilt, Scottish shoes and jacket, and a Sikh turban.

New confidence

In spite of all this, the majority of Scots people enjoy a good quality of life. Scottish standards of health care and education are higher than elsewhere in the UK. Like other British citizens, most Scots can afford comfortable homes, leisure-time entertainments and enough to eat. They believe that Scotland is a great place to live!

Famous Scots

Most famous Scots have been exceptionally tough, determined and independent-minded. They have fought for what they wanted, or what they believed to be right. Yet each made their own unique, individual contribution to Scotland's story.

Heroes and Villains

There were some dreadful wrongdoers in Scotland's past – and lots of brave, good people. But many famous Scots were heroes and villains, all at the same time.

Their enemies said they were wicked and dangerous. But their supporters claimed they were fighting for justice and liberty.

Lord Montrose created Scotland's first national army by leading royalist Scots from many parts of the country to fight against the Roundheads.

James Graham, Lord Montrose (1612–1650)

From a noble family, Montrose fought for the Scottish Covenanters (Presbyterian Protestants) against the English king, Charles I. But he opposed the Covenanters' plans to ally with the English Roundheads (Protestant republicans) and changed sides. He was made King Charles's Lieutenant (deputy) in Scotland and won six battles against the Roundheads. But in 1646 he was defeated and forced to escape to Norway. In 1649 he returned to Scotland but was captured the next year and executed (by the Roundheads) without trial.

William Wallace (around 1274–1305)

Wallace was born near Paisley. In 1297, he was outlawed by English armies after he killed the English Sheriff of Lanark. In return, Wallace burned Lanark, then led the Scottish army to victory against the English at the battle of Stirling Bridge. Appointed Guardian of Scotland, he led many more attacks on England. But in 1298 he was defeated at the battle of Falkirk and fled to France. He returned to Scotland in 1303 but was betrayed, captured, put on trial by the English, then brutally executed.

Did you know?
Born in Largs, Fife, Alexander Selkirk (1676–1721) ran away to sea. He was marooned on a Pacific island, where he survived alone for over four years until rescued in 1709. His bravery and resourcefulness inspired Daniel Defoe to write the novel "Robinson Crusoe".

William Kidd (around 1645–1701)

Originally from Greenock, Kidd became a ship owner in New York. The English king, William III, licensed him to fight pirates in the Indian Ocean. But "Captain Kidd" became a pirate himself, and captured many rich prizes. He was arrested in America, sent back to England and hanged.

Pirate-chaser Captain Kidd became a pirate himself and paid the price with his life!

Rob Roy, "Red Rob", Robert MacGregor (1671–1734)

Roy was born near Stirling. After fighting for the Jacobites in 1689 he became a wealthy cattle-dealer. But in 1712 some of his workers ran away, taking money Roy owed to the Duke of Montrose with them. In revenge, the Duke seized Roy's land and had him made an outlaw. From then on, Roy lived by stealing cattle and sheep, and blackmailing landowners. He also fought in the Jacobite rebellion of 1715. He escaped many attempts to capture him but was finally arrested in 1727. The king pardoned Roy and he lived the rest of his life in peace.

Outlaw and Jacobite rebel, Rob Roy's courage made him a hero.

More Heroes and Villains

The famous Carnegie Hall, New York, named after Andrew Carnegie who founded the building.

Flora MacDonald (1722–1790)

From South Uist in the Hebrides Isles, MacDonald was adopted as a child by a Jacobite noble family. In 1746 she smuggled Bonnie Prince Charlie to safety from the Scottish mainland to the Isle of Skye after the failed Jacobite rising of 1745. As a punishment, she was imprisoned in the Tower of London, but later pardoned and freed. In 1774, she emigrated with her husband to America, but later returned to Scotland, where she spent the rest of her life.

Andrew Carnegie (1835–1918)

Born in Dunfermline, Carnegie emigrated to the USA and made an enormous fortune in oil, iron and steel. He gave most of his money away to good causes, including international peace, and to schools, universities and libraries in Scotland.

Thomas Glover (1838–1911)

Nicknamed "the Scottish Samurai", Glover was the son of a coastguard in Fraserburgh. He travelled to China aged 19, then sailed to Japan in 1859, learned Japanese and became a successful trader. He joined Japanese samurai (elite warriors) in a rebellion against the Shogun (ruling army commander). In 1870, he joined the new, fast-growing Mitsubishi company, and set up a brewery. He ended his life as a wealthy and respected businessman, honoured by the Japanese emperor.

Thomas Glover was a businessman, who fought alongside Japanese rebels. He studied Japanese history, especially the stories of past samurai warriors.

Douglas Haig, Lord Haig (1861–1928)

Son of an Edinburgh businessman, Haig became a professional soldier, fighting bravely in Sudan and South Africa. Clever but unpopular, from 1915 to 1918 he commanded the British army in France, during the First World War. Haig's battle plans (which were strongly criticized) led to the death of over one million men, but eventually won the War. When the War was over, Haig worked to help ex-soldiers. He started the annual Poppy Day appeal, and was the first president of the new British Legion.

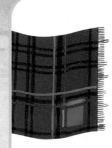

Did you know?

Allan Pinkerton (1819–1894) was born in Glasgow but he emigrated to the United States of America, where he became Sheriff of Chicago. He later founded his own very successful private detective agency, which became world famous.

Haig, in army uniform, standing in front of First World War graves.

Donald Caskie (1902–1983)

Nicknamed "the Tartan Pimpernel", Caskie was minister of the Scottish Church in Paris, France. During the Second World War, he risked his life to help British servicemen escape the Nazis. He was tortured and sentenced to death, but he was set free thanks to a German clergyman.

Scientists and Engineers

Scottish engineers and inventors made the Industrial Revolution possible. Throughout the 18th and 19th centuries, they invented new machines and new processes that changed the way goods were made.

They also greatly improved transport – especially roads, canals and railways. This helped British manufacturers to get their goods to market, and British merchants to play a leading part in international trade.

James Watt (1736–1819)

Watt began his career as a scientific instrument maker. While working at Glasgow University in 1763, he was asked to mend a model steam engine designed by English inventor Thomas Newcomen. Watt realized it could be made much more efficient, and began to design steam engines of his own. They were the best yet made, but for many years he could not afford to develop them. Then, in 1774, Watt arranged a partnership with English businessman Matthew Boulton. Together they made steam engines to pump water from mines and to power spinning and weaving machines.

This dramatic portrait, painted in 1825, shows James Watt watching an experiment to produce steam.

The Menai Suspension Bridge (seen in the background) was built by Thomas Telford, and opened in 1826.

Thomas Telford (1757–1834)

Telford trained as a stonemason and studied architecture. He won great praise for his work on canals in England and Wales before returning to Scotland in 1802. There, his task was to survey transport in the Highlands and improve it. Between 1803 and 1847, he designed and built the Caledonian Canal (it linked the North Sea with the Atlantic Ocean) together with over 1,400 km (900 miles) of new roads and 1,200 new bridges.

> ### Did you know?
> *Robert Stevenson (1772–1850) designed and built over 20 lighthouses in remote, dangerous places. Stevenson also invented the bright flashing light that worked inside his lighthouses.*

James Neilson (1792–1865)

After working at Glasgow Gas Works, Neilson studied air and gas scientifically. In 1828, he pioneered a new method for smelting iron ore. It used heated air and became known as the "hot blast" process. It was very successful and allowed iron to be produced from Scottish coal and stone more quickly, cheaply and efficiently than before.

Bell Rock lighthouse, off the east coast of Scotland, designed by Stevenson in 1807.

Sir William Thomson, Lord Kelvin (1824–1907)

Born in Belfast, Thomson moved to Glasgow as a child, and entered university there when he was only 11 years old. During his long career, he made many important discoveries about heat, movement, electricity and magnetism. He worked out a new way of measuring temperature – the Kelvin Scale – and became famous for over 50 inventions. These included insulated cables (used to send messages by newly invented telegraph) and a compass for use at sea.

1767	1787	1810	1812	1816	1818
James Small patents the chain plough.	Andre Meikle designs the world's first threshing machine.	John McAdam builds the first weather-proof road surfaces.	Henry Bell builds steamship *Comet* to operate steamboat passenger service.	David Brewster invents the kaleidoscope.	Thomas Wilson launches the first iron passenger ship.

Inventors

Alexander Graham Bell (1847–1922)

Bell began his career in Edinburgh as a teacher of people with hearing difficulties. In 1870 he left Scotland for Canada and the USA. There, he set up a school and studied the science of speech. This led him to try sending spoken messages along telegraph wires and, in 1876, he transmitted a few words from one room to another. This was the first telephone call!

Bell opens the first telephone service between New York and Chicago in 1892.

John Logie Baird (1888–1946)

After training as an electrical engineer, Baird became fascinated by the idea of sending pictures, as well as words, along wires. In 1926 he built a simple television transmitter and receiver but it took him 10 years to produce good-quality pictures. At first, Baird's television broadcasts were in black and white but he finally produced colour broadcasts shortly before he died.

Sir Robert Watson-Watt (1892–1973)

British government scientist Watson-Watt was an expert on radio waves. He realized they might be used to locate the position of planes as they flew through the air. In 1935 he invented a system that he called "radio detection and ranging", or radar. It could identify aircraft 160 km (100 miles) away and warn that they were approaching. During the Second World War, radar helped defend Britain from enemy attack, and saved many lives.

Sir John Napier in his study, painted in 1616.

Kirkpatrick Macmillan rode his invention 112 km (70 miles) from his home village to Glasgow.

Kirkpatrick Macmillan (1813–1878)

Born to a farm labourer's family, Macmillan worked as a blacksmith. He experimented by building three-wheeled, pedal-powered machines, then designed the first two-wheeled bicycle in 1839. It was very heavy and had wooden wheels. Once news of Macmillan's new bicycle spread, many other inventors copied his designs.

Scottish Inventors

1823	1825	1828	1839	1863	1888	1958
Charles MacIntosh patents waterproof cloth.	James Chalmers invents gummed postage stamps.	Patrick Bell invents mechanical reaper (corn cutter). Robert Wilson invents screw propeller.	James Nasmyth invents steam hammer.	James Clerk Maxwell discovers the theory of magnetic waves.	John Dunlop invents pneumatic (air-filled) rubber tyres.	Ian Donald discovers use, in industry and medicine, for ultrasound waves.

Doctors and Nurses

Scotland has a long history of medical expertise. By 1495 there was a medicine teacher at Aberdeen University. In the 17th century there were guilds of physicians and surgeons in Scottish towns.

Scotland's first medical school opened in Edinburgh in 1726 and its first training hospital in 1729. During the 19th and 20th centuries, Scottish doctors pioneered new treatments and discovered drugs that saved millions of lives.

Sir James Simpson (1811–1870)
Simpson was Professor of Midwifery at Edinburgh. He experimented with anaesthetics to ease pain in childbirth. At first he was criticized but his treatment was accepted after Queen Victoria became his patient in 1843.

Joseph Lister, Lord Lister (1827–1912)
Professor of Surgery at Glasgow, Lister studied the work of the French scientist, Louis Pasteur. From this, he learned that infections are caused by invisible bacteria (germs). In 1867 Lister sprayed operating rooms with carbolic acid, which killed germs and stopped infections. Soon, other surgeons copied Lister's technique.

This early photograph, taken around 1860, shows Sir James Simpson in his consulting room.

Discoveries in Medicine

1745
James Lind experiments with lemon juice to treat scurvy (a disease caused by lack of fresh fruit and vegetables).

1766
James Lind travels to China to investigate Asian diseases.

1880s
Sir William MacEwen invents "aseptic" methods of operating – dressings and instruments were sterilized in boiling water.

Elsie Inglis (1864–1917)

Until the late 19th century, women in Scotland could not be doctors. To help them, Inglis set up the Medical College for Women in Glasgow, and a women's hospital in Edinburgh. At the start of the First World War (1914), Inglis volunteered to be an army doctor but was rejected. So she recruited her own women doctors and nurses. They cared for soldiers and civilians in many parts of Europe – even though they were often arrested as spies.

Inglis proved that women could work as doctors, even in tough wartime conditions.

Alexander Fleming (1881–1955)

During the First World War, Fleming was shocked to see soldiers dying from wounds infected by germs. He decided to search for drugs to fight infection. In 1928, he noticed how mould in a dish was killing germs, but could not collect enough of it to be useful.

In 1939, the Second World War began, and more soldiers died from infections. Then scientists Ernst Chain and Howard Florey remembered Fleming's work. They made a drug, penicillin, from the mould he had described. It was the first antibiotic; many people called it a miracle.

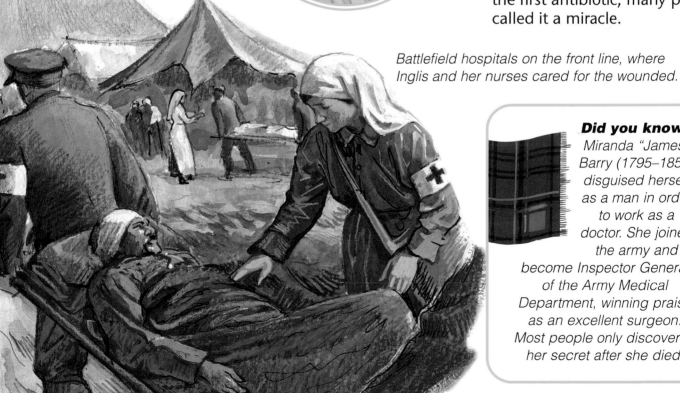

Battlefield hospitals on the front line, where Inglis and her nurses cared for the wounded.

Did you know?
Miranda "James" Barry (1795–1856) disguised herself as a man in order to work as a doctor. She joined the army and become Inspector General of the Army Medical Department, winning praise as an excellent surgeon. Most people only discovered her secret after she died.

1894
Sir Patrick Manson discovers that malaria is carried by mosquitoes.

1902
Sir Ronald Ross wins Nobel Prize, also for work on malaria.

1957
Alexander Todd (Lord Todd) wins Nobel Prize for work on vitamins, human cells and DNA.

Columba became Scotland's favourite saint. This picture was painted to honour him almost 1,500 years after his death.

People of God

Scotland's religious leaders have always been keen to take action – to spread news of their faith, reform church teachings or change the world. These religious leaders have often caused controversy, and sometimes died for their beliefs.

St Columba (AD521–597)

Columba belonged to a royal family in Donegal, Ireland. He became a monk and trained as a writer and artist. But he also fought in battles and this led to his exile from Ireland in AD563. He fled to Iona, an island off western Scotland. He built a monastery there, then travelled throughout Scotland to convert its different peoples to Christianity.

John Knox (1513–1572)

Knox studied at St Andrews University, and became a Catholic priest. But he soon joined Scottish Protestants, who were calling for church reform. In 1546 he was imprisoned for his beliefs, then forced to row French galleys (ships) as punishment. Once freed, he fled to England, then to Geneva (Switzerland), where he wrote a book complaining about Catholic women rulers, especially Scotland's Mary of Guise.

In 1559 he returned to Scotland to help set up the new, Presbyterian Church. When Mary Queen of Scots came to power, Knox again risked punishment by criticizing her Catholic faith and her behaviour.

David Livingstone (1813–1873)

From Blantyre, near Glasgow, Livingstone was sent to work in a cotton mill, but studied in his spare time. Aged 24, he left to train as a doctor and study Christianity. In 1841 he went as a medical missionary to South Africa. From there, he travelled north, exploring the Zambezi River. In 1855 he was the first European to see the mighty Victoria Falls.

In 1856 Livingstone returned to Britain, but soon went back to Africa to campaign against the slave trade. In 1866 he made another expedition to Africa, to search for the source of the River Nile. Presumed lost, he was "discovered" in 1871 by journalist Henry Morton Stanley.

Livingstone braved mighty rivers, tropical diseases and lions while exploring Africa.

Mary Slessor (1845–1915)

Born to a poor family, Slessor began work aged 11 in a jute factory in Dundee. She became a Christian missionary in 1875 and was sent to Nigeria, in Africa. There she lived simply, alongside local people, helping them, teaching them and studying their language and traditions. Although church superiors disapproved of her way of life, Slessor was respected by ordinary villagers, who called her "Mother".

Mary Slessor arrived in West Africa in 1876. She improved the position of African women in society and is today regarded as one of Africa's pioneers in women's rights.

> ### Did you know?
> Eric Liddell (1902–1945) worked as a Christian missionary in China – and he was also a great athlete. He won a gold medal in the 400 metres at the 1924 Paris Olympics. Liddell refused to race on Sundays because of his religious beliefs. The award-winning film "Chariots of Fire" tells the story of his life.

Artists and Designers

Throughout Scotland's history, men and women have created many beautiful things – from prehistoric stone circles and gold jewellery to Celtic crosses and medieval churches.

Sadly, most of their names have not been recorded. But here are some examples of creative Scottish people from more recent times.

Robert Adam (1728–1792)

Born in Kirkcaldy, Fife, Adam was the son of an architect and was trained by his father. As a young man he travelled through Europe, studying old buildings and archaeology. In 1761 he became Architect of the King's Works – a very important position. From 1769 he worked, with his brother James, to build elegant houses for rich families throughout Britain. His buildings were based on ancient Greek and Roman designs, and often decorated with delicate plasterwork.

Culzean Castle, designed by Robert Adam in 1777.

Artists of Modern Times

James Guthrie (1859–1930)
Member of the "Glasgow Boys" group of artists, who painted scenes from everyday life.

Samuel Peploe (1871–1935)
Influenced by French artistic styles, his works experimented with effects of colour, light and shade.

Anne Redpath (1895–1965)
Famous for abstract paintings that celebrated everyday objects and Scottish landscapes.

Allan Ramsay (1713–1784)

Scotland's first great painter, Ramsay was the son of a well-known poet and librarian. As a child he showed skill at drawing, so his father sent him to Europe to study art. From 1738 Ramsay worked mostly in London, where he became famous for painting wonderful portraits. But he also spent time in Edinburgh, where he founded the "Select Society", a discussion group for clever, interesting people, in 1745.

Sir Henry Raeburn (1756–1823)

An orphan, Raeburn trained to be a goldsmith in Edinburgh, and taught himself to paint in his spare time. He invented his own special way of working, using broad, bold brushstrokes, and dramatic contrasts of light and shade. Many rich and powerful people paid him to paint their portraits.

Sir Henry Raeburn, painted around 1815.

This elegant wooden chair was designed by Charles Rennie Mackintosh.

Charles Rennie Mackintosh (1868–1928)

Born in Glasgow, Mackintosh trained as an architect and also studied at Glasgow's famous School of Art. There, he met and married designer Margaret Macdonald. They worked together on many projects, helping to create a new "Glasgow Style" in art and craft. It was influenced by the latest European trends – and very unpopular in Britain. Later, Mackintosh developed his own experimental designs for buildings and furniture, based on tall, thin shapes and straight lines. They looked stunning, but were often not very comfortable. He spent his last years as a painter.

Eduardo Paolozzi (born 1924)

Creates bright, colourful images inspired by technology and popular music.

Elizabeth Blackadder (born 1931)

A teacher at Edinburgh School of Art for several years; awarded many honours; famous for her pictures of flowers.

Jack Vettriano (born 1951)

Vettriano left school at 16 to work in the coalfields. Paints glamorous men and women in mysterious settings.

Poets and Novelists

Scotland has a long history of story-telling. Celtic bards, medieval minstrels and many ordinary men and women at Highland ceilidhs (gatherings) all entertained their listeners with dramatic tales and ballads (stories in song).

After around 1700, many poems and stories were written down and published as books, so we know their authors' names. Here are just some of the most famous.

Robert Burns (1759–1796)

Scotland's best-loved writer, Burns came from a poor family in Ayrshire. He worked, unsuccessfully, as a farmer, then became a government tax official. He wrote passionate, dramatic and very entertaining poems in Lowland Scots. More than any other writer, he was able to describe what ordinary Scottish people felt about life. A handsome, witty, charming young man, he became a great celebrity in Edinburgh after his first poems were published. He also became famous for his many romantic affairs.

Sir Walter Scott (1771–1832)

Son of an Edinburgh lawyer, Scott also studied law. He loved the traditional songs and stories of the Borders region where he was born, and these inspired him to become a writer. He translated German poems, then composed many of his own, on romantic Scottish themes. He published his first novel, *Waverley*, a Scottish historical adventure, in 1814, and it was an overnight success. Scott also set up a publishing company but it failed and he lost all his money. He worked extremely hard, writing many more books to pay off his debts. Sadly, the effort killed him.

Influential Writers

William Dunbar (1460–1513)

Worked at the court of James IV. His poems were satirical, romantic and clever.

Alasdair MacMhaighstir Alasdair (1695–1770)

Teacher; wrote in Gaelic. His poems supported the Jacobites, and describe adventures at sea.

William McGonagall (1830–1902)

Sometimes called "the World's Worst Poet", McGonagall travelled through Scotland giving readings. People liked to laugh at him and he became very popular.

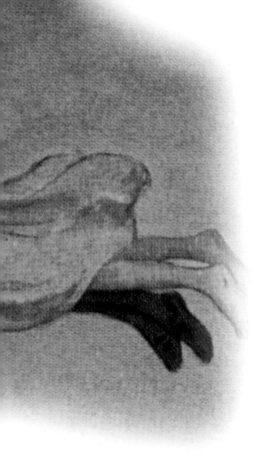

In J M Barrie's very popular play, Peter Pan and Wendy can fly.

Sir J M Barrie (1860–1937)

From a weaving family in Angus, Barrie went to Edinburgh University, then worked in England as a journalist. His first successful book, *A Window in Thrums*, described everyday Scottish life. But he became better-known for writing plays, especially the magical *Peter Pan*, first performed in 1904.

Sir Arthur Conan Doyle (1859–1930)

Born in Edinburgh and trained as a doctor, Doyle wrote to support himself during the early years of his career. His most famous creation was the detective, Sherlock Holmes. Doyle's books became popular but he continued to work as a doctor, caring for soldiers with great bravery during the Boer War (1899–1902). He also worked as a war correspondent during the First World War (1914–1918).

(left) This romantic portrait of a romantic poet shows Robert Burns in the Scottish countryside.

The adventures of Conan Doyle's detective, Sherlock Holmes, and his friend, Dr Watson, have entertained millions of readers all round the world.

Kenneth Grahame (1859–1932)
Famous for children's stories, especially *The Wind in the Willows*.

Dame Muriel Spark (born 1918)
Writes biographies, poems and thought-provoking novels. Most famous book: *The Prime of Miss Jean Brodie*.

Irvine Welsh (born 1961)
Writes disturbing novels about modern Scottish city life. Most famous work: *Trainspotting*.

Liz Lochhead (born 1947)
Best known for warm, honest, witty writing, using everyday language. Many poems look at women's lives.

Writers and Thinkers

After around 1600, most Scottish children had the chance of a basic education, and a fortunate few went to excellent schools and universities.

From around 1700, well-educated Scots were among the leading writers and thinkers of their time. Scottish writers also used their works to criticize society, or put forward political ideas.

Hume's revolutionary ideas about our minds and religion shocked many people of his own time, and they are still studied today.

David Hume (1711–1776)

Born in Edinburgh, Hume worked as a junior government minister. But he achieved much greater praise – and blame – for his books on philosophy. His most famous works, such as *An Enquiry Concerning Human Understanding* (1748), investigated how our minds work and how we know about the world. His ideas were not understood in Britain but were eagerly accepted in France. Hume also wrote on politics and economics, and caused a scandal by refusing to believe in God.

John Buchan's spy novel, "The Thirty Nine Steps", features mysterious secret agents, romantic railway journeys and dramatic chases across wild, Scottish countryside.

Adam Smith (1723–1790)

Educated at Glasgow and Oxford universities, Smith became Professor of Moral Philosophy at Glasgow in 1752, then tutor to the sons of the Duke of Buccleuch in 1763. Three years later, Smith retired to his birthplace, Kirkcaldy, and spent 10 years writing *An Enquiry into the Nature and Causes of the Wealth of Nations* – one of the world's most important books on politics and economics. Smith's ideas still influence some conservative politicians today, but are unpopular with most socialists.

James Boswell (1740–1795)

Son of a Scottish lord, Boswell studied law in Glasgow and Edinburgh, then ran away to London, hoping to join the army. He became close friends with famous writer and scholar Dr Samuel Johnson, and in 1773 toured the Scottish Highlands and Islands with him. He is remembered today for his descriptions of this journey and of Johnson – and also for his personal diaries, which vividly record his own thoughts and feelings.

John Reith, Lord Reith (1889–1971)

Born in Stonehaven, the son of a church minister, Reith trained as an engineer. In 1922 he became manager of the newly founded British Broadcasting Corporation (BBC), then Director-General in 1927. A forceful character, Reith held strong views about broadcasting, and these shaped BBC programmes for many years. He believed that radio (and later television) should inform and instruct (teach) listeners and viewers, not merely entertain them.

John Buchan is most famous for his exciting stories describing the adventures – and beliefs – of the perfect "British Empire" hero.

Did you know?

John Buchan (1875–1940), who later became Baron Tweedsmuir, was a lawyer, an MP, a writer, a soldier and a publisher! He was also Governor-General of Canada. His most famous work, "The Thirty Nine Steps", was published in 1915.

Political People

Many of Scotland's most inspiring politicians have supported unpopular causes – from the Act of Union to Communism. But they have all had the courage to stand up for what they believed to be right.

The Duke of Argyll controlled the government of Scotland and appointed his supporters to government jobs.

Hardie helped create new Labour (socialist) parties in Scotland and England.

Archibald Campbell, Duke of Argyll (1682–1761)

Politician, lawyer and soldier, Campbell backed plans to unite Scotland to England in 1707. Rich, and from an old noble family, he had so much power that people called him "the uncrowned king of Scotland".

Keir Hardie (1856–1915)

The son of a ship's carpenter, Hardie began work aged 7. At 10 years old he became a coal miner. He studied in his spare time and organized miners' campaigns for better pay and conditions. He was sacked, then found work as a journalist and trades union official. In 1888 he was founder chairman of the new Scottish Labour Party, and in 1892 became a Labour MP. In 1893 he was chosen to be leader of the new UK Independent Labour Party. In 1914 he tried to organize strikes by trades unions throughout Europe to protest at the First World War. He died, disappointed, the next year.

Rebels and Campaigners

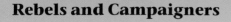

Viscount "Bonnie" Dundee (1649–1689)

Rebel; led Jacobite Highland clans against Mary II and William of Orange. Killed at battle of Killiecrankie.

Henry Dundas, Lord Melville (1742–1811)

Member of UK Parliament, Lord Advocate (chief Scottish law officer), Home Secretary, Treasurer to the Navy and Governor of the Bank of Scotland.

Patrick Colquhoun (1745–1820)

Glasgow merchant, magistrate and campaigner for law and order.

James Ramsay MacDonald (1866–1937)

MacDonald trained as a teacher, then moved to London where he became active in socialist politics. In 1900 he was appointed secretary of the Independent Labour Party. In 1906 he became a Labour MP, but lost his seat in 1918 after opposing the First World War. He was re-elected to Parliament in 1922, and was chosen as leader of the Labour Party. In 1924 he became Prime Minister in Britain's first Labour government, but lost office after a year. He was Prime Minister again during the years of global economic crisis, from 1929 to 1935. In 1931 he agreed to lead a coalition government with members from different political parties. Many Labour supporters saw this as a betrayal.

James Ramsay MacDonald angered most of his old Labour Party supporters but stayed in power to serve his country at a difficult time.

Katharine, Duchess of Atholl (1874–1960)

Wife of a noble landowner, the duchess was a talented musician. In 1923 she stood as a Conservative candidate in the General Election and became the first Scottish woman to be elected to the UK Parliament. The next year, she was chosen to be the first British female cabinet minister. She took a special interest in education, poverty and social inequality, and worked to help disadvantaged children throughout the British Empire. She was also an outspoken anti-fascist campaigner, and resigned her seat in Parliament when Britain signed an agreement with Hitler's Germany in 1938.

Alexander Macdonald (1821–1881)

Coal miners' trade union leader. One of first two working men elected to UK Parliament in 1875.

Clementina Black (1853–1922)

Campaigned for decent wages and working conditions for women; also women's right to vote.

Tom Johnston (1882–1965)

Minister in Churchill's government during Second World War. Tried to rebuild Scottish industry.

Modern Politicians

Twentieth-century politics in Scotland was dominated by leaders from socialist and liberal parties. But it also saw the growth of a new movement, calling for Scottish independence.

John Smith (1938–1994)

From the west of Scotland, Smith studied law at Glasgow University. He became a Labour Party MP in 1970. A brilliant speaker and clever debater, he was admired for his performances in the UK Parliament, and served as an opposition "shadow" minister. In 1992 he was elected leader of the Labour Party and tipped as a future Prime Minister, but died suddenly. His loss was mourned by politicians from all parties.

Donald Dewar (1937–2000)

Born in Glasgow, Dewar became a lawyer then a Labour Party MP. He held several Opposition posts but was always happiest in Scotland. He was respected as an honest, caring, intelligent – and eccentric – politician. In 1997 Dewar became Secretary of State for Scotland in the new Labour government. He guided Scottish devolution arrangements, but opposed Scottish independence. He became First Minister in the new Scottish Parliament in 1999, but died suddenly, and unexpectedly, in 2000.

Donald Dewar takes part in a debate at a Labour Party conference in Scotland.

Twentieth-century Politicians

Arthur James Balfour (1848–1930)

Conservative member of UK Parliament and Prime Minister 1902–1906. Promised Jewish people a homeland – Israel.

John Maclean (1879–1923)

Campaigned tirelessly to turn Scotland into a workers' republic. Was imprisoned for protesting against First World War. Set up new Scottish Workers' Party.

Winnie Ewing became President of the Scottish National Party (SNP) in 1987.

Tony Blair (born 1953)

Born in Edinburgh, Blair trained as a lawyer. In 1983, he became a Labour Party MP and was soon given important posts as a member of the Opposition. In 1992 he became Labour Party leader, introducing many new policies and organizational reforms. His "New Labour" Party won large majorities in the General Elections of 1997 and 2001. Blair worked hard to negotiate a peace plan for Northern Ireland, and allowed votes on devolution for Scotland and Wales. In 2002–2003 he was criticized for his support of American foreign policy, especially during the Iraq War.

Jennie Lee (1904–1988)

The daughter of a miner, Jennie Lee was a feminist and equal opportunities campaigner. She became a Labour MP in 1929, Minister for Arts in 1964 and later founded the Open University.

At 24, Jennie Lee was the youngest member of the House of Commons. She continued to campaign for workers' rights until 1970, when she retired.

Winnie Ewing (born 1929)

First Scottish National Party MP, elected 1967. Later, a member of European Parliament (1975) and Scottish Parliament (1999).

Jimmy Reid (born 1932)

Born in Glasgow slums, became trade union officer and leading member of Communist Party. Campaigned to save Clydeside shipyard jobs.

David Steel, Lord Steel (born 1938)

Liberal Democrat politician at Westminster, social reformer; first Presiding Officer of the new Scottish Parliament.

Lynch was a brilliant boxer but he found the pressures of fame too much to bear.

Sporting Stars

Scottish sports stars have a proud record of achievement.

They have won many championships in sports originating in Scotland, such as golf and curling, and have also succeeded in international competitions.

Tom Morris (1851–1875)

Born in St Andrews, the home of Scottish golf, Morris came from a famous golfing family. His father (also called Tom Morris) designed golf courses and won championships. "Young Tom" was the most remarkable golfer of his time. In 1868 he was the youngest player to win the Open Championship – then won it again for the next three years! Morris died tragically, aged only 24. Many people believed that he would have achieved still greater success, had he lived.

Benny Lynch (1913–1946)

Born in a rough, tough district of Glasgow, Lynch was a wild youth and became involved with criminal gangs. Always keen on boxing, he decided to train as a professional. He won many fights and, in 1935, became the first Scot to win a World Boxing Championship, as a featherweight. But he developed a problem with alcohol abuse, lost fights, became ill and died young.

Football and Rugby Heroes

Sir Matt Busby (1909–1994)

Manager of Manchester United. He showed courage in rebuilding his team after he was injured and many of his young footballers were killed in an air crash at Munich in 1958.

Bill Shankly (1913–1981)

Football manager. Led Liverpool to win UEFA cup in 1973. Inspired much affection as well as respect.

Jock Stein (1922–1985)

Football manager. Led Glasgow Celtic to many victories, including European Cup in 1967 and 1970. Also led Scottish national team to World Cup finals in 1982.

Jackie Stewart (born 1939)

Born into a motor-racing family in Dunbartonshire, Stewart was also a talented target-shooter. He drove in his first Grand Prix race at Monza, Italy, in 1965 – and won! He was World Champion driver in 1969, 1970 and 1973, then retired to work as a radio and TV commentator, and to campaign for improved safety standards in motor sport. He trained – and inspired – many young Scottish drivers.

Top goal-scorer Dalglish, one of Scotland's most respected soccer stars.

Kenny Dalglish (born 1951)

Honoured as the greatest Scottish footballer of the 20th century, Dalglish played for Glasgow Celtic and Liverpool. He was capped for the Scottish national team 102 times, and was the first player to score 100 goals in English and Scottish football. In 1985 Dalglish became a football manager, leading teams in England and Scotland.

Bill MacLaren (born 1925)

Sports commentator on radio and TV. Greatly admired as "the Voice of Rugby".

Sir Alex Ferguson (born 1941)

Manager who led Manchester United to win the "treble" in 1999; they won the FA Cup, the Premier League and the European Champions Cup.

Andy Irvine (born 1951)

Captain of Scottish rugby team, also played for British Lions. First player to score more than 300 points in international career.

More Sporting Stars

Sir Peter Heatly (born 1924)

Champion diver Heatly won the Scottish title a record-breaking 21 times. He also took gold medals for Scotland in the Commonwealth Championships of 1950, 1954 and 1958. He later followed a successful career in sports management. His responsibilities included bringing the Commonwealth Games to Edinburgh in 1986.

Jim Clark (1936–1968)

Born in Fife, Clark drove in his first race aged 20. In 1960 he took part in his first Grand Prix race. It was the start of a record-breaking career. Clark won 25 Grand Prix titles and, in 1963, became the youngest driver to win the World Championship. He won the same championship in 1965, also the Indianapolis 500 title – the first non-American to do so. Clark was tragically killed in a practice race in Germany in 1968.

Clark's brilliant career was cut short by a high-speed crash.

MacInnes climbed Everest in 1972 and 1975. He has since gone on to design new mountain safety equipment to help the climbers of today.

Hamish MacInnes (born 1930)

Mountaineer MacInnes made important climbs in the Alps, the Caucasus, New Zealand, South America and the Himalayas. He was part of the first team to traverse the treacherous Cuillin range on the Island of Skye in winter, in 1965. He also pioneered mountain rescue techniques, especially using dogs.

Sporting Honours

Bobby Thomson (born 1924)

Baseball player who emigrated to the USA. Nicknamed "the Flying Scot". Won 1951 National League Championships.

Willie Carson (born 1942)

Champion flat-race jockey, in 1977 appointed "Jockey to the Queen".

Richard Noble (born 1946)

Holder of world land-speed record; leader of "Thrust" team that reached 1,229 kph (763 mph) in 1997.

Sir Charles "Chay" Blyth (born 1940)

Born in Hawick, the youngest of seven children, Blyth worked in a weaving mill, then joined the army. In 1966, with John Ridgeway, he rowed across the Atlantic Ocean in 90 days. In 1971 he became the first yachtsman to sail single-handed, non-stop round the world. Since then, Blyth has won many races at sea and set up a successful yachting adventure company.

Hendry has become one of the most successful snooker players of all time.

Stephen Hendry (born 1969)

Born in Edinburgh, snooker player Hendry became the youngest-ever World Champion in 1990. Since then, he has won the same championship a record-breaking six times, and collected a further 66 titles.

Liz McColgan (born 1964)

Distance runner, winner of gold medals at Commonwealth Games in 1986 and 1996, silver medal at Olympics (1988) and London Marathon (1996).

Fiona MacDonald (born 1974)

Youngest member of Scottish women's curling team (with Rhona Martin, Janice Rankin, Debbie Knox, Margaret Morton). Gold at Winter Olympics 2002.

John Higgins (born 1975)

Snooker player. Winner of World Championship 1999.

Entertainers

Scots have always enjoyed a good time! But we do not know the names of harpists and bards who played for ancient Scots kings, nor of ordinary Scots villagers who made their own entertainment, telling stories at ceilidhs, playing fiddles for dancing, or making *port a bheul* (mouth music).

Since the 19th century, there have been many well-known Scottish entertainers performing in theatres and music halls. Modern films, radio and television have also made them famous worldwide.

Harry Lauder's good-humoured performances encouraged the Scots to relax and laugh at themselves.

Sir Harry Lauder (1870–1950)

Lauder worked in coal mines as a child, before winning a singing contest. Dressed in exaggerated Scots style – with a kilt, huge "bonnet" (hat) and knobbly walking stick – he created a music-hall act that was popular throughout the UK and in the USA. He wrote many songs and encouraged audiences to sing along with him.

Sir Sean Connery (born 1930)

For a while, young Connery worked as a milkman. Then success in body-building competitions helped him win a small part in a London musical. This led to a television acting appearance and several film roles. Connery's great breakthrough came in 1962, when he played glamorous spy James Bond – and became a star. He made seven Bond films and many others, winning Academy Awards (Oscars) in 1987 and 1990.

Sean Connery, in his most celebrated role as James Bond.

Billy Connolly (born 1941)

After a miserable childhood, Connolly trained as a welder in Glasgow shipyards. He also played the banjo and sang in folk clubs, telling jokes between songs. These were so popular that Connolly became a full-time comedian, appearing on stage and television in Britain, the USA and Australia. His quick, sharp wit – and willingness to shock – won him many fans. He was also praised for serious acting roles and for supporting charities.

Scottish entertainers also include cartoon characters. The most famous is Dennis the Menace, who has appeared for over 50 years in "The Beano", a children's comic produced by Scottish publisher D C Thomson.

Ewan McGregor, one of Scotland's latest acting stars to hit the big time in Hollywood.

Did you know?
Ewan McGregor's uncle, Denis Lawson, is also an actor and starred in the first three "Star Wars" films. Ewan recently starred in the "Star Wars" prequels himself.

Evelyn Glennie (born 1965)

Percussion-player Glennie showed musical skill from a young age, even though she became deaf aged 12. After studying in London, she travelled to learn more about music from different cultures – and how to play an astonishing range of instruments. Glennie's brilliant performances, warm personality, energy and enthusiasm have won great admiration worldwide and inspired many composers to create works for her.

Index

Index

Radical Wars 140
Raeburn, Sir Henry 173
railways 125, 133
Ramsay, Allan 121, 173
rationing 149
record-breakers 184–5
red grouse 114
Redpath, Anne 172
referendums 154, 155
Reformation 85
Reid, Jimmy 181
Reith, Lord 177
religion
    early pagan rituals 15
religious reform 47, 54, 55, 90–1,
    141
    see also Catholic Church; Celtic
    Church; Christianity; Church in
    Scotland; Druids; Protestantism
rent strikes 139, 144
Rheged 31
Rizzio, David 92
road construction 125, 165
Rob Roy (Robert MacGregor) 161
Robert I (Robert Bruce) 66–7, 70
Robert II (Robert the Steward) 71,
    72
Robert III 73
Romans 26–7, 28, 30, 32
Ross, Sir Ronald 169
roundhouses 20–1
rugby 183
Ruthven Raid 94

S

St Andrews 47, 85, 170
saints *see* Columba; Kentigern;
    Margaret; Ninian
Saltire 152
Sauchieburn, battle of 77
schools 84–5, 121
science and engineering 122–3,
    125, 132, 133, 164–7
"Scots": origin of name 30
Scots National League 154
Scott, Sir Walter 130, 174
Scottish Enlightenment 120–1
Scottish Home Rule Association 154
Scottish Mercury 113
Scottish National Orchestra 153
Scottish National Party 154, 155
seals 53, 57
Second World War 146–7, 148, 149,
    154, 163
Selkirk, Alexander 160
Shankly, Bill 182
sheriffs 63, 118
Sherrifmuir, battle of 117
Shetland 35, 48, 49, 77

shielings 61
shinty 85
ship-building 132, 133, 142, 151,
    165, 181
shooting estates 126, 142
Simpson, Sir James 168
Skara Brae 13
Skye 139, 184
slave trade 17, 115
Slessor, Mary 171
Small, James 165
Smith, Adam 177
Smith, John 180
snooker 185
social problems 157
socialism 144, 147, 178
Solway Moss, battle of 89
Somerled 49, 78
song schools 84, 85
South Uist 15
Spark, Dame Muriel 175
sport 152, 182–5
stagecoach services 125
Standard, battle of the 59
standing stones 15
steam power 123, 124, 125, 132,
    164, 167
steamboats 123, 125, 138, 165
Steel, Lord 181
Stein, Jock 182
Stevenson, Robert 125, 165
Stewart dynasty 72, 76, 77, 78
Stewart, Alexander ("Wolf of
    Badenoch") 72
Stewart, Charles Edward ("Bonnie
    Prince Charlie") 118, 119, 162
Stewart, Jackie 152, 183
Stewart, James Edward ("Old
    Pretender") 109, 116, 117
Stirling Bridge, battle of 65, 160
Stirling Castle 88
stone circles 14–15
stone crosses 33
Stone of Scone (Stone of Destiny)
    43, 154, 155
Strathclyde 31, 35
Sweetheart Abbey 91
Symington, William 123
Synod of Whitby 33

T

tacksmen 61, 80
tartan *see* plaid
taxes 36, 51, 57, 70, 71, 75, 86, 113,
    155
telephones 166
television 153, 166
Telford, Thomas 125, 165
tenements 134, 135

textile industries 122, 124, 125, 132
Thomson, Bobby 184
Thomson, Sir William (Lord Kelvin)
    165
Thorfinn the Mighty 49
timber industry 150
tin 16, 17
Todd, Alexander (Lord Todd) 169
tools, early 11, 12, 13, 16
tourism 152, 156
tower-blocks 149, 150
town councils 57, 85, 95, 140, 141
towns 56–7, 71, 113, 150, 151
trade 17, 19, 48, 56, 63, 81, 82, 115
trades unions 140, 141, 144, 150,
    178, 179, 180
tramways 125
Tudor, Margaret 87
turnpike roads 125
tweed 138

U

unemployment 144, 145, 149, 153
union of Scotland and England
    116–17, 118
United Free Church 141
universities 85, 153

V

Vettriano, Jack 173
Victoria, Queen of England 131
Vikings 34–5, 36, 37, 40, 41, 42, 44,
    48, 49
voting rights 140, 141, 179

W

Wallace, William 65, 66, 160
Watson-Watt, Sir Robert 167
Watt, James 123, 164
weapons 16, 17, 19, 23, 53
welfare state 148
Welsh, Irvine 175
whisky 115
Whithorn 54
William the Conqueror 44, 45, 52,
    59
William I 59
William II of England 59
William III of England 110, 116, 117
Wilson, Robert 167
Wilson, Thomas 165
Wishart, George 91
witchcraft 77, 102–3
working classes 133, 134–5, 140,
    144
written records 36, 51

Y

yachting 131, 185

ACKNOWLEDGEMENTS

Illustrations :

James Field: 10, 16, 19, 20–21, 25, 27, 30, 32, 40–41, 42, 47, 48, 52–53, 58, 60, 61, 64, 66, 70, 72–73, 75, 76, 77, 78–79, 81, 82, 94, 101, 105, 107, 111, 115, 117, 127, 133, 139, 146, 150, 154, 162, 165; Chris Forsey: border and additional map art; Mike Lacey: 12–13, 14–15, 18, 22–23, 28, 29, 34, 36, 37, 45, 46, 50, 54, 55, 56, 59, 63, 65, 67, 71, 83, 84–85, 87, 89, 91, 93, 95, 97, 102–103, 109, 112, 113, 116–117, 118, 120, 122, 125, 140, 143, 149, 152, 176–177, 179, 181, 182, 184–185, 186; Chris Molan: 130, 134, 135, 137, 144, 145, 161, 167, 169, 171, 172, 175; Ian Thompson: 6–7, 11, 26, 31, 35, 78, 100, 119.

Photographs (t = top, (m) = middle, (b) = bottom):

Bridgeman Library: Board of Trinity College Dublin/Bridgeman Library 31; Musée de la tapisserie, Bayeux, France/Bridgeman Art Library 44; Castle Museum and Art Gallery, Nottingham, UK/Bridgeman Library 96. **British Library:** © By permission of the British Library; Roy.2.B.VII f78v/51, SLOANE.3983 f5/57, COTT.VIT.A.XIII f4v/59, COTT.VIT.A.XII f6/63. **British Wool Marketing Board:** © Picture courtesy of British Wool Marketing Board 126. **Corbis:** Yogi Inc/Corbis 151, Macpherson Colin/Corbis Sygma 180, Macpherson Colin/Corbis Sygma 181, JP Laffont/Sygma/Corbis 183, Bettman/Corbis 186. **D C THOMSON:** © D C Thomson & Co Ltd, 2004 187. **EMPICS:** © EMPICS 307139 183. **Historic Scotland:** © Crown copyright reproduced courtesy of Historic Scotland SkaraBrae22/13, CAL.1–00120/14, MaesHowe/15, ELG.1–000650/29, HS84/30, ION.1–000322/33, ABE.2–000015/37, MIEGLE–NO2/41, EDI.1–002036/43, EDI.1–000551/45, DUN.4–000089/47, Jarlshof3/49, BOT.1–000139/53, HS99/55, cow/61, Wallace/65, DOU.3–00128/73, Linlithgow Pal2/74, EDI.1–000452/76, Holyrood/86, Falkland Palace/88, sweetheart2/91, LochlevanAerial4/93, JamesVI/94, Duf.2–000077/112, Forth Bridge/133, G6427 3/137. **Kelvingrove Art Gallery**: © Glasgow Museums: The People's Palace 114. **Mary Evans Picture Library**: © Mary Evans Picture Library 10013260/80, 10073061/81, 10121713/83, 10067669/84, 10020418/102, 10018803/103, 10023626/106, 10023648/107, 10057094/108, 10102213/111, 10136748/114, 10011316/116, 10018269/119, 10143853/121, 10025727/123, 10121606/125, 10016644/131 (b), 10010536/131 (t), 10130945/138, 10023022/140, 10048868/141, 10089218/143, 10094835/161, 10094308/163, 10073847/165, 10015887/166, 10086504/169, 10022043/174–175, 10072101/177, 10044608/178. **Mary Slessor:** Mary Slessor Foundation 171. **National Archives of Scotland:** GD45/13/216 National Archives of Scotland 51, © SP13/7 National Archives of Scotland 67, © GD40/12/2 National Archives of Scotland 104. **National Library of Scotland:** © The trustees of the National Library of Scotland Andrew Myllar, Printer's Device/85, Gordon Highlanders/142. **National Museums of Scotland:** © The trustees of the National Museums of Scotland 11, X.AF 1097.1&2/12, Beaker pottery 17 (t), H.KL 54/19, 23, X.FV 27/27, H.KE 14/33 (t), 35, 41 (m), K.1999.733/53 (t), K.1999.828/57 (t), K.1999.747/71, 73 (t), 78, H.KL 19/88 (t), © the Singh Twins, Amrit and Rabindra K.2000.621 D/157, H.SBV 8/173 (b). **National Portrait Gallery:** © National Portrait Gallery, London NPG 541/96, NPG 843/104, NPG 531/109, NPG 1902/110 (t), NPG 197/110 (m). **New Lanark Trust:** © New Lanark Conservation Trust 124 (m); 124 (b). **North Lanarkshire Council:** © North Lanarkshire Council Museums and Heritage Service 150. **Rex Features:** © Clive Dixon/Rex Features 162, SIPA Press/Rex Features 184, Robin Hume/Rex Features 185. **Royal Commission on the Ancient and Historical Monuments of Scotland:** © B11Y36 Crown copyright Royal Commission on the Ancient and Historical Monuments of Scotland 17. **Royal Shakespeare Company:** © The Murder of Duncan, "Macbeth", by George Cattermole (1850) reproduced courtesy of the Royal Shakespeare Company 43. **Scottish Crannog Centre:** © Scottish Trust for Underwater Archaeology/24. **Scottish Life Archive:** © The trustees of the National Museums of Scotland C20157/132, 62/47/32A/135, C24082/136, C18275/138 (m), C10233/145, C6945/147 (t), Dalmuir/147 (b), C25811/148 (t). **Scottish National Portrait Gallery:** © Scottish National Portrait Gallery; Adam de Colone, James VI & I/100; Antonio David, Prince Charles Edward Stuart/118 (t); Unknown, James IV/87; Unknown, James I/74; Unknown, Mary Queen of Scots/92; Richard Wilson, Flora Macdonald/ 118 (b); Willem van Honthorst, Lord Montrose/160; Unknown, John Napier of Merchiston/167; Willem Hole, St Columba/170, Sir James Simpson/168, Alexander Nasmyth, Robert Burns/174; Allan Ramsay, David Hume/176; Allan Ramsay, 3rd Duke of Argyll/178; © National Gallery of Scotland; Allan Ramsay, The Artist's Wife/121; © Benjamin West, Alexander III of Scotland Rescued from the Fury of a Stag by the Intrepidity of Colin Fitzgerald/62; James Eckford Lauder, James Watt/164. **St Giles' Cathedral:** © St Giles' Cathedral, 1990. **The Scotsman:** © The Scotsman Newcraighall/148, li295631b/153, li328601b/155, li328641b/155, pd2342193b/156–157, li29734b/156, li171905b/187. **William Thornton:** © William Thornton 152.